Hana Coufalová

Marketing Strategy for Medical Devices

Hana Coufalová

Marketing Strategy for Medical Devices

New Product Launch

LAP LAMBERT Academic Publishing

Impressum/Imprint (nur für Deutschland/only for Germany)
Bibliografische Information der Deutschen Nationalbibliothek: Die Deutsche Nationalbibliothek verzeichnet diese Publikation in der Deutschen Nationalbibliografie; detaillierte bibliografische Daten sind im Internet über http://dnb.d-nb.de abrufbar.
Alle in diesem Buch genannten Marken und Produktnamen unterliegen warenzeichen-, marken- oder patentrechtlichem Schutz bzw. sind Warenzeichen oder eingetragene Warenzeichen der jeweiligen Inhaber. Die Wiedergabe von Marken, Produktnamen, Gebrauchsnamen, Handelsnamen, Warenbezeichnungen u.s.w. in diesem Werk berechtigt auch ohne besondere Kennzeichnung nicht zu der Annahme, dass solche Namen im Sinne der Warenzeichen- und Markenschutzgesetzgebung als frei zu betrachten wären und daher von jedermann benutzt werden dürften.

Coverbild: www.ingimage.com

Verlag: LAP LAMBERT Academic Publishing GmbH & Co. KG
Heinrich-Böcking-Str. 6-8, 66121 Saarbrücken, Deutschland
Telefon +49 681 3720-310, Telefax +49 681 3720-3109
Email: info@lap-publishing.com

Herstellung in Deutschland:
Schaltungsdienst Lange o.H.G., Berlin
Books on Demand GmbH, Norderstedt
Reha GmbH, Saarbrücken
Amazon Distribution GmbH, Leipzig
ISBN: 978-3-8383-5484-2

Imprint (only for USA, GB)
Bibliographic information published by the Deutsche Nationalbibliothek: The Deutsche Nationalbibliothek lists this publication in the Deutsche Nationalbibliografie; detailed bibliographic data are available in the Internet at http://dnb.d-nb.de.
Any brand names and product names mentioned in this book are subject to trademark, brand or patent protection and are trademarks or registered trademarks of their respective holders. The use of brand names, product names, common names, trade names, product descriptions etc. even without a particular marking in this works is in no way to be construed to mean that such names may be regarded as unrestricted in respect of trademark and brand protection legislation and could thus be used by anyone.

Cover image: www.ingimage.com

Publisher: LAP LAMBERT Academic Publishing GmbH & Co. KG
Heinrich-Böcking-Str. 6-8, 66121 Saarbrücken, Germany
Phone +49 681 3720-310, Fax +49 681 3720-3109
Email: info@lap-publishing.com

Printed in the U.S.A.
Printed in the U.K. by (see last page)
ISBN: 978-3-8383-5484-2

CONTENT

ACKNOWLEDGEMENT 5

INTRODUCTION 7

AIM OF THE BOOK 9

1   THEORY 11

   1.1   MARKETING 11

   1.2   INTERNATIONAL MARKETING 11

   1.3   MARKETING STRATEGY 13

      1.3.1   Company Position in the Market 15

      1.3.2   Competitive Strategies 15

   1.4   PLANNING PHASE 17

      1.4.1   Situation Analysis 17

         1.4.1.1   SWOT Analysis 17

         1.4.1.2   PEST Analysis 18

      1.4.2   Goal Setting, Product and Market Focus 19

         1.4.2.1   Segmentation and Targeting 20

         1.4.2.2   Positioning 22

      1.4.3   Marketing Plan 24

         1.4.3.1   Marketing Mix 24

         1.4.3.2   Product Life Cycle 35

         1.4.3.3   Marketing Communications Budget 36

   1.5   IMPLEMENTATION PHASE 37

   1.6   CONTROL PHASE 37

      1.6.1   Current Results – Evaluating, Interpreting and Improving 38

      1.6.2   Marketing Effectiveness Audit 39

2   COMPANY OVERVIEW 40

   2.1   ST. JUDE MEDICAL, INC. 40

   2.2   COMPANY DEVELOPMENT 41

   2.3   PRODUCTS 42

   2.4   FOCUS AREAS GROWTH 43

      2.4.1   Atrial Fibrillation 43

      2.4.2   Cardiac Rhythm Management 44

2.4.3 Neuromodulation...45

2.4.4 Cardiovascular...45

2.5 COMPANY STRUCTURE..46

3 ANALYTICAL PART **48**

3.1 STRUCTURE OF BCC...48

3.2 CARDIAC ABLATION...49

3.3 PRODUCTS TO BE LAUNCHED..50

3.4 CREATION OF A NEW PRODUCT LAUNCH PLAN 50

3.4.1 Starting Point...52

3.4.2 Analysis Of The Current Situation..52

3.4.2.1 PEST Analysis 53

3.4.2.2 SWOT Analysis 57

3.4.2.3 Objectives 59

3.4.2.4 Segmentation and Targeting 60

3.4.2.5 Positioning 60

3.4.2.6 Messaging 61

3.4.3 Marketing Launch Plan 62

3.4.3.1 Activities of Departments 64

3.4.3.2 Marketing Mix 66

3.4.3.3 Medical Device Life Cycle 70

3.4.3.4 NPL Budget 71

3.4.4 Implementation and Control Phase 71

4 STRATEGY PROPOSAL **73**

4.1 CRITICAL POINTS...73

4.1.1 Marketing/Marcom...74

4.1.1.1 Marketing Management 74

4.1.1.2 Marketing 75

4.1.1.3 Marcom 76

4.1.2 Education..76

4.1.3 Clinical 77

4.1.4 Legal, Regulatory, Quality Affairs & Business Development............................77

4.1.4.1 Legal 77

4.1.4.2   Regulatory 77

4.1.5   Operations/Capital Equipment Service 78

4.1.5.1   Operations 78

4.1.5.2   Service.. 79

4.2   PROPOSITIONS 79

4.3   FORECASTED COSTS AND GAINS 84

CONCLUSION.. **88**

REFERENCES **90**

LIST OF USED ABBREVIATIONS **93**

LIST OF APPENDIXES.. **94**

APPENDIXES **94**

ACKNOWLEDGEMENT

I would like to thank to the supervisor of the book to Ing. Vít Chlebovský, Ph.D., next to the employees of the company St. Jude Medical, especially to Pablo Castrosin del Mazo and Kris D'hulst, for willingness and assistance with the elaboration of this book.

INTRODUCTION

In today's market, it is very important to have a good and detailed marketing to be able to succeed. Every marketing plan is different depending on the product, the company and the situation on the market. Everybody who attended at least a basic marketing course should be able to imagine what would be a marketing plan like for consumers' good, e.g. clothes or food. However, the creating of a marketing plan for medical devices, which are high-tech and specialized products sold on a high competitive market, can be more challenging.

The book is based on the author's experience gained during her internship at the Atrial Fibrillation marketing department of the EMEAC (Europe, Middle East, Africa, Canada) Headquarters of the American company St. Jude Medical in Brussels. The author participated on the creation and implementation of the new product launch plan there and found out that in the process is still a space for improvement. Due to that the author chose the topic Marketing Strategy for Medical Devices Market and set the aim of the book to optimize a launch plan strategy.

The aim will be achieved by three separate but related steps. The first step is to describe the creation of the launch plan for the European Union market. The creation of the plan is the responsibility of the Atrial Fibrillation marketing manager who works for the EMEAC Headquarters in Brussels. The second step is to carry out an analysis of the entire process of creation and implementation of the launch plan in order to identify critical steps that have to be ensured to avoid delays or cancellations of the launch. The final step leading to optimization of the process is to propose improvements of the product launch within the European Union and specify the forecasted costs and gains of the suggested solutions.

The creation of the marketing plan of medical devices is very important and complex issue. St. Jude Medical launches more than forty products per year and that is the reason why it is important for them to continually improve and adapt the process to constantly changing conditions on markets. The book will help the company to realize the important steps during the launch procedure and propose possible solutions for current problems that can also occur in the future if they are not taken care of.

AIM OF THE BOOK

The aim of the book is to optimize a launch plan strategy on the European Union market for products of the Atrial Fibrillation portfolio of the American company St. Jude Medical.

The applied methods that will help to achieve the above mentioned aim are the analysis of the external environment (the PEST analysis), the analysis of the internal environment (the SWOT analysis) and the Four Ps Framework (Product, Price, Place, Promotion). All these methods are described in a greater detail in the theoretical part of the book.

1   THEORY

1.1   MARKETING

Marketing is a very quickly developing discipline and that is why it is very important for a company to be flexible enough in following new trends, which can change from day to day, and following customer needs, which are gradually higher and higher.

In the old times, the economy was based on the Industrial Revolution, on managing manufacturing industries and the business was limited by political and trade barriers. Contrary to the industrial society, today's post-industrial economy has witnessed "the digital revolution" where the management of information about customers, products, prices, competitors, and every other aspect of the marketing environment has come to play a vital role. The data is being analyzed in a very short period of time and business is being done on the global market place. The revolution has placed also a whole new set of capabilities in the hands of consumers and businesses – such as a substantial increase in buying power (price and product attributes comparison, purchase making), a greater variety of available goods and services, information about practically anything or placing and receiving orders anywhere.

Today's marketing goal is not only to increase market share, profitability or gain further customers at the expense of the direct competition, but also to have a long-term strategic development based for example on a strategic partnerships developed on an international level. Regarding the medical industry, it is very important to maintain good relationships with customers – so-called relationship marketing, which is a part of Customer Relationship Management. This helps to create a series of one-to-one, long-term, profitable relationships between a company and its customers. (16, 20)

1.2   INTERNATIONAL MARKETING

"International marketing is a business philosophy focused on satisfying the needs and wishes of customers in international markets. The main goal of an international marketing strategy is to create maximum value for stakeholders by optimizing a firm's resources and searching for advantageous business opportunities in foreign markets." (20, p. 8)

International marketing has some features in common with the domestic marketing however there many specifics that have to be taken into consideration when choosing a marketing strategy. These specifics can become a great advantage and bring lots of new opportunities or can become a threat for a company. Some of the specifics, which the international marketers have to face, are listed below:

- legislation;
- regulation;
- trade and political barriers;
- conditions for business activities of foreign companies;
- global marketing network;
- strategic alliances;
- social and cultural differences and their influence on the behavior and decisions of customers;
- a good quality survey of new foreign markets is difficult;
- preference of domestic products and producers;
- organization of the foreign markets
- problems with entering distribution channels;
- adapting the marketing mix;
- working in and unfamiliar environment
- facing different lifestyle;
- language barriers and other. (20, p. 9)

On the one hand, going across borders brings many new opportunities, which can generate profit, if a company is successful. It can as well help to diversify the risks. A company is then no longer dependant only on one market and that brings certain flexibility in decision-making. That is why going international can be also used as a tool of risk management.

On the other hand, international marketing faces many various risks. A company should try to minimize the risks as much as it can but from the obvious reasons connected to the national markets differences listed above, it can never completely avoid them. Among the risks, we can define:

- Political risks (nationalization and monetary restrictions, war, strikes, terrorism, natural disasters);
- transfer risks (money transfer disturbed by government by freezing the money outflow from the economy);
- country risks (stability of a country, macroeconomic changes);
- commercial risks (reliable business partner in foreign country);
- financial risks (exchange rate risks, interest risks). (20)

1.3   MARKETING STRATEGY

A strategy in general is a plan about how to get from one place to the other desired place. However, no plan can be developed without a proper preparation. First, a company has to realize where it is now and where does it want to go in the future. For management this means taking strategic decisions about the company's mission and the width of its domain (e.g. types of industries, product lines). Knowing the starting point and the final point allows a company to think about how to get there. The choice of the ways to get to the final point can be limited by financial and human resources and that is the reason why a company needs to know how to obtain and allocate its resources. Another important factor of success of the plan is to know how a company will compete with its competitors and how it can position itself to get a sustainable advantage. Having the research done and the plan developed a company can start translating the plans into actions. To see if the plan is working well a company should control the results of the implementation in comparison with its plans and eventually make some corrections to the original plan.

The same approach is used in a *strategic marketing process* although it goes more into detail. A company allocates its marketing mix resources to reach its target markets. This process consists of three main phases: the planning, implementation, and control phase. (For more information see picture nb. 1).

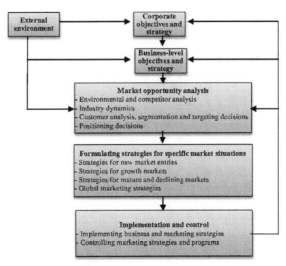

Picture 1: The Process of Formulating and Implementing Marketing Strategy (25, p. 26)

The strategic marketing process is formalized in a ***marketing plan*** that specifies all the marketing activities in a certain time frame (usually long term and annual periods) in order to reach the defined marketing goal, which must be consistent with other business goals of the company to improve the total performance. The marketing plan should be simple, to the point and respecting the design of the brand, product plan, market segment and geographical plan. It has to contain at minimum: situation analysis, marketing objectives and goals, marketing strategy (including the marketing mix and the marketing budget), marketing action plan and marketing controls. There are several ***types of marketing plan***:

- Brand marketing plan (for brands);
- product category marketing plan (for each product category, includes brand marketing plan);
- new product plan (very detailed launch plan);
- market segment plan (when product is sold to different segment, plan is prepared for each segment);
- geographical market plan (for country, region, city);
- customer plan (for each valued customer). (3, 17, 25)

14

1.3.1 Company Position in the Market

As already mentioned in the previous chapter, no matter which type of a plan a company is developing, it has to realize where it is now – on which *position in the market* – to know what possibilities it has. They can vary according to the market attractiveness and company's power.

Attractive Market – Strong Company

If a market is very attractive and a company is one of the strongest in the industry then it can invest available resources to support the offering.

Attractive Market – Weak Company

If a market is very attractive but a company is one of the weaker ones in the industry then it should focus on strengthening the position to reach its goal.

Not Especially Attractive Market – Strong Company

If a market is not especially attractive, but a company is one of the strongest in the industry then it should use an effective marketing and sales efforts to create profits in the near future.

Not Especially Attractive Market – Weak Company

If a market is not especially attractive and a company is one of the weaker ones in the industry then the company should continue with promotion of the offering only if it supports other more profitable part of the company's business. (4)

1.3.2 Competitive Strategies

A very important aspect mentioned above is that a company knows how to compete with its competitors and how to position itself to get a sustainable advantage. There are many possible competitive strategies that a company can use but the three basic ones are low-cost leadership strategy, differentiation strategy and focus strategy:

Low-Cost Leadership Strategy

It is based on the ability of a company to produce a good quality product or service in large volumes at low costs, lower than its competitors cost, and market them for competitive prices. A company sells a good value for budget prices. This strategy requires standardized products, which means producing only a few models with limited optional features. A company has the ability to set a floor on market price but the low costs should create profit margins that are higher than the industry average thanks to the high volume of production. To keep this strategy a company should have an on-going availability of operating capital, good engineering skills, close management of labor, products designed for an ease of manufacturing and low cost distribution.

Differentiation Strategy

This strategy is based on offering a product or service that is different from what the competition offers. The production consists of many models, options and services and can be perceived as unique. This strategy is usually used by companies from developed countries, which offer value-added products for higher prices. The value can stand for brand image, technology, special features, superior service, a strong distributor network and so on. The strategy is suitable especially for technologically sophisticated products, biotechnologies, services and branded consumer goods. The higher prices should create higher profit margins, higher than the industry average margins. To create and maintain this strategy a company should have strong marketing abilities, effective product engineering, creative personnel and a good reputation and constantly look for innovations.

Focus Strategy

It is a strategy of market niche that is used when the two previous strategies are not appropriate. The number of buyers is very limited as the product or service is specialized and quite expensive. It is designed to address a certain segment in the market and serve the segment in the way that other companies cannot compete. This strategy is typical for producers of luxury goods or of special equipment for certain industrial branches. The market is small as well as the number of customers but thanks to specialization, high prices and minimal competition a company can create very high margins. (4, 20)

In the following chapters, the different components of a marketing plan will be discussed one by one in a greater detail to understand the strategic marketing process better.

1.4   PLANNING PHASE

The planning phase of the strategic marketing process consists of a market research and a situation analysis, goals setting and a development of a marketing plan. These features will be discussed in the next chapters.

1.4.1 Situation Analysis

A major factor in the success or failure of a marketing strategy at any level is whether it fits in the market environment and if the offering meets the requirements of potential customers. That is the reason why the marketing manager must first monitor and analyze the opportunities and threats caused by factors outside the company and secondly analyze the company itself – its strengths and weaknesses. An honest and detailed evaluation of external and internal factors is the key element in creating a successful marketing strategy. Marketing managers can use various types of analysis but the most known are the SWOT analysis and the PEST analysis.

1.4.1.1 SWOT Analysis

On the one hand, a SWOT analysis is an analysis of the internal factors of the company. It should be an honest appraisal of the strength and weaknesses of the firm that are critical factors in the development of the strategy. These factors show the company on which aspects it can build its future success and on which aspects it should work to improve them.

S – Strengths (brand name, product features, good reputation, product quality, company sales, market shares)

W – Weaknesses (less known brand, higher costs, less innovative product)

On the other hand, SWOT is also an analysis of the external factors outside the company. The marketing managers must understand potential opportunities and threats over the long term and predict them, know the strengths and weaknesses of the competitors to be able to get a sustainable competitive advantage.

O – Opportunities (market niche, weaker competition, growing market)

T – Threats (competitive product, new strategy of competition, slowing down market)

1.4.1.2 PEST Analysis

The second analysis model is the PEST analysis. This model is particularly useful for international companies, because they operate in various markets. As these markets can be very different, the company should analyze the differences to be able to adjust its strategy to local conditions. However, in searching for information, a company can make two mistakes – either get too much or too little information. To figure out these errors a company should develop a model of those factors that primarily drive its sales, costs, and profits. The model on which a company management bases its decision can vary for every company. A company can use secondary data that were already collected for another purpose and/or primary data, which a company gathers itself. Companies create their own models of analysis, which can be based on the general analytical tool for a basic analysis of the international environment known as PEST.

P – Political, legal and regulatory environment
E – Economic environment
S – Social and cultural environment
T – Technological environment

Political, legal, and regulatory environment:
- Legislation;
- regulatory environment (regulations, deregulations can open/close market, destabilize industries, change revenue potential, safety regulations);
- tariffs, quotas, customs, administrative entry procedures, requirements and restrictions on the quality, packaging, labeling, procurement policies, export subsidies, local content laws, import restrictions, taxes, price controls;
- licensing;
- lobbying.

Economic/Demographic environment:
- Economic well-being (GNP, exchange rates, distribution of income by age);
- education;
- population;
- demographic trends, age, geographical groups and other.

Social and Cultural environment:

- Consumer information important for demand, advertising, product positioning, package design;
- values, beliefs, and norms of individuals in a given society;
- fashion, lifestyle trends.

Technological, Competitive and Infrastructure Environment:

- Structure of the industry;
- emerging technology;
- information about competitors (their objectives, strategies, strengths, weaknesses and response patterns);
- collaboration information;
- geographical location;
- special conditions (extreme temperatures, high humidity; can affect the design and demand of products);
- channels of distribution;
- local transport system;
- media. (16, 17, 20)

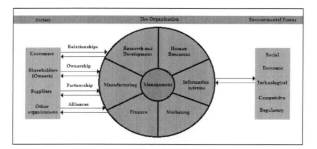

Picture 2: External and Internal Factors of the Company (3, p. 10)

1.4.2 Goal Setting, Product and Market Focus

After the first analysis's (SWOT, PEST and other) are done, a marketer will shift his interest towards the development of a marketing plan. However to be able to start developing the marketing plan, a company first has to set a feasible objective and a goal, which it wishes to reach. ***Objectives*** are usually broad and tell what should be achieved in the coming period (e.g. increase market share) on the other hand ***goals*** states a size and a target date of objectives (e.g. Increase market share from 15 to 15 percent by the end of the quarter four this year). Without setting a goal marketers would not know which direction to go and which steps to take. A plan that is made without a goal would not have many chances to succeed. The goal has to be defined by a number and by time frame and has to be consistent with the company strategy. Usually companies wish to reach a certain level of profitability measured in for example return on investment, return on assets, marginal contribution, cash flow, and market share.

To succeed in a very competitive marketplace a company should have a certain competitive advantage, which it can get by knowing its consumers very well. Finding the specific target groups and having all available information about them is crucial. Without it, marketers would not know to whom they should address the offering. Customers play a central role in a marketing plan, as a company is dependent on them. They are the ones who bring their wants and needs and it is a company's job to try to satisfy them in order to generate a profit. To choose the customers to who the offering will be addressed, a company uses methods called segmentation and targeting. These methods are discussed in the next chapter. (17, 25)

1.4.2.1 Segmentation and Targeting

Every market consists of groups (segments) of customers with different needs and wants. Normally no company tries to sell to everyone and that is why it has to find its targeted groups of customers and find as much information about them as possible.

In international marketing the targeting is very similar to the targeting on domestic markets, it is only more complicated because of a lack of available data for marketing research and possible political risks. A company used to see a country as a single segment in global market segmentation but nowadays companies are more and more determining homogeneous groups of consumers across countries. (25)

We can divide market into three levels – brand segment level, the niche level, and the market cell level.

Brand Segment Level

Markets can be broken down into the following broad segments of customers:

- Benefit segmentation (buyers who look for similar benefit, e.g. low price, high quality, excellent service);
- demographic segmentation (buyers who share a common demographic makeup, e.g. young low-income minorities);
- occasion segmentation (buyers who use product under certain occasion, e.g. airline passengers flying for business or pleasure);
- usage level segmentation (buyers who are heavy, medium or light users or nonusers of the product);
- lifestyle segmentation (buyers grouped by lifestyle).

After identification of the different segments in a market, every marketer hopes to recognize an unmet need that might represent a profitable market opportunity. He can focus on only one segment (single segment marketing) or two or more segments (multisegment marketing).

Single segment marketing – on the one hand, buyers can be more easily identified, their needs are easier to be met which gives competitive advantage. On the other hand, this creates risk that the segment will become smaller or will attract too many competitors. From this reason, most of the companies prefer multisegment marketing.

Multisegment marketing – offering to different segments lower the risk of smaller profit if one segment would be weaker and it gives a cost advantage. (16,17, 20)

The Niche Level

Niches usually consist of less customers who have more narrowly defined needs or unique combinations of needs. Advantages of offering to this segment are: there is less competition, better knowledge of the customer, and a high margin because customers are willing to pay more for such a specialized product that meets their needs. The disadvantage is the possibility that the segment could become smaller and, if it would be the only segment the company is focused on, it could force the company to leave that market. (17, 20)

The Market Cells Level

A market cell is even a smaller group of customers than a niche. Companies are trying nowadays to gather every available information about the specific cell (e.g. customers' demographics, past purchases, preferences, or postcode). (17)

Segmentation and targeting are the key elements to create the right positioning of the product, as will be discussed in the next chapter.

1.4.2.2 Positioning

After making the marketing research a company will probably find several customer segments (which were described in more detail in the previous chapter) that could be suitable for the specific product. However, the management has to target the segment that will bring the biggest profit and focus on this segment. Depending on the market segment the company is aiming for, the management must create the position of the offering. The positioning, supported also by the marketing mix (the four Ps), has to meet the needs of the target customers and show them at first glance the core benefits of the product. The positioning can be divided into several groups:

- *Attribute positioning* (company positions itself on some feature, e.g. oldest restaurant in the city, but this feature does not bring any benefit to the customer);
- *benefit positioning* (the product promises a benefit);
- *use/application positioning* (product is positioned as the best in certain application, e.g. sport shoes for running, for playing football, basketball);
- *user positioning* (product is positioned for a certain group, e.g. Apple computer is the best for graphic designers);
- *competitor positioning* (product is different and better than the competitor's one);
- *category positioning* (company describes itself as a category leader);
- *quality/price positioning* (product is positioned at a certain quality and certain price level). (17, 20)

As Kotler says: "Positioning is the effort to implant the offering's key benefit(s) and differentiation in the customers' minds". (17, p. 56)

Usually companies advertise only a single major benefit positioning (e.g. best quality, safest, fastest, most prestigious, best performance). However, well chosen positioning should present not only the core benefit but also other additional benefits which will together answer potential buyers' question why to buy exactly this product. That is why some companies add also the second or even the third benefit positioning.

The key is not to present as many core benefits as possible but to choose the right benefits that suit the targeted consumers' need. In case something goes wrong and the positioning is not well chosen, it can present a serious problem to the company and it can stop a company from reaching the planned profits. Moreover, the company may risk a huge loss of customers. Wrong positioning includes:

- *Underpositioning* (underestimating the product's benefits);
- *overpositioning* (overestimating the product's benefits);
- *confused positioning* (contradictory benefits)
- *irrelevant and doubtful positioning*.(fictitious benefits). (16, 17, 20)

So far, this chapter was about how to position a product when it is clear who is the end user and usually the end user is also the buyer. Positioning for medical devices is more complicated because there are three different segments with different needs. The producer is the medical company and the final user is the patient but there are still two other very important sides that need to be taken into account –the physician and the management of the hospital which employs the physician. All of these sides have different needs and wants. To find a compromise between these contradictory needs is the most important and the most difficult task of medical companies and their sales representatives.

CUSTOMER	NEED
Patient	To be cured.
Physician	To have the latest hi-tech technology there is, to perform as well as possible.
Management of hospital	To provide a good quality care for a reasonable price.

Table 1: Conflict between Different Needs in the Medical Industry

1.4.3 Marketing Plan

A Marketing plan consist of situation analysis, marketing objectives and goals, marketing strategy (including the marketing mix and the marketing budget), marketing action plan and marketing controls. All these features will be described in the following chapters.

1.4.3.1 Marketing Mix

The concept of marketing mix was originally invented by Professor Jerome McCarthy in early 1960s as a four P framework (product, price, place, and promotion). Later marketers started to criticize this model arguing it was not mentioning other important things such as services, packaging, personal selling, politics, or public opinion. However, nowadays whether marketers take into account 4Ps or more Ps, they can still use this framework as a tool that can guide them in marketing planning. (17)

In an international environment, marketing managers have to create even more detailed plan than for the domestic launch to be able to cover all the differences. Key is to know to what extent the four P elements of marketing plan can be standardized. Standardization helps to create savings mainly on manufacturing and on marketing costs. It is not possible to standardize everything, of course there will be differences in pricing due to various parameters as: manufacturing, marketing costs, taxes, and the prices of competitive products. There will also be differences in advertising because of cultural and language differences that require adjustments. However, all the adjustments must be consistent and integrated in the marketing strategy. There are three options for a company:

- *Adaptation* (companies should not decide for either standardization or a localization strategy but combine the two, the objective should be to obtain a similar response and not to use the identical advertising across countries = "Plan global, act locally");
- *Use of International Media* (international print media, or international TV channels, but they are limited by programming, regulated use of ads, and lower rates of TV ownership in poor countries);
- *Personal Selling* (companies can use either independent agents, hire its own sales force, or combine the two but difficulties may appear with organizing the selling efforts across borders, nevertheless the companies which are selling complex high-

tech products (computers, medical devices, pharmaceuticals) need to employ sales representatives and preferably their own sales representatives). (25)

In the following part, the four Ps (Product, Price, Place, and Promotion) which are the basis of every marketing plan will be discussed in greater detail.

PRODUCT (Product Offering)

A product offering is the basis of every business. Every company tries to make its offering in some way stronger and better (in a relevant way) and different from its competitors to draw the attention of potential buyers. The offering can differ in the following features:

- Physical differences (product variety, quality, size, features, packaging, design, brand name);
- availability differences (available on the internet, in stores, possible to order by phone);
- service differences (training, repair, delivery, service, warranties);
- price differences (high or low price);
- image differences (symbols, reputation, media). (16, 17)

In general, we can divide all the products in two big categories: the differentiable products and commodities.

Differentiable products differ mainly in physical terms by features, design, size, materials, style and so on (cars or buildings). Marketers can use for these kinds of products also a psychological differentiation like prestige or safety.

However, there are *commodities* that are very difficult to differentiate. They are all over the world the same and that is why they can be diverse only to some point. Among these offerings, we can include for example metal, salt, fruit and vegetables. They can be differentiated in either real terms (place of origin, image, or reputation) or in psychological terms when the differentiation is often made only in the customers' minds (e.g. very similar taste of various types of vodka, or different types of cigarettes).

In addition, for leading companies it is important to have an *innovative approach* to differentiate a product –whether it is a commodity or a differentiable product. An innovative approach means that new features are highlighted. These features are meant to provide added benefits to the products if compared with the competition. It has to be noted however that sooner or later, any successful offering will be imitated. This fact can cause problems for a company producing the original because the *imitation* is usually sold at a lower price. The company can either lower the price to keep their market share, but accept lower profits, or keep the price on the same level and loose some market share and profits. An alternative approach would be to find a new feature that could differentiate the product resulting in an equal market share whilst keeping the current price. Nevertheless, a company should constantly look for advantages to set a sustainable and long-lasting business. (17)

When a company sells its offering both on the domestic market and abroad in international markets, it not only has to make a decision about how to differentiate its products but it also has to decide on how to accomplish this in the different markets. To do this, the company can adopt either a standardized or a localized *international marketing strategy*. Before deciding this, a detailed research has to be done to gather important information on which strategic decisions can be based. For example, it is important to know the conditions of usage of the product in each country. In any case, the offered product has to be of good quality as recently it has become a must for a company to be quality certified. (25)

In the international marketing strategy, usually we have to adjust the offering. More specifically, we can adjust offering's three dimensions – a core (physical and technical dimension), services (packaging and service), and symbolic values (brand name and image):

- *Adjustment of the core* means development of a country specific product (different product for each country or group of countries, this affects a big part of total costs);
- *Adjustment of the services* means adaption of a product to local conditions (minor changes in packaging, color, or voltage for example, this affects only a small percentage of total costs);
- *Adjustment of the symbolic values* means to sell the same product in all countries (only labeling and language manuals differ, customer needs are perceived as the same, the most preferable option with almost no additional costs). (20, 25)

PRICE

Price is the only element of four Ps that creates revenue – the other Ps create only costs. That is the reason why companies try to set the price as high as the level of differentiation allows them. Pricing includes list prices, discounts, allowance, payment period, credit terms and other. The company has to base the setting of the price on many aspects, as it is a very complex issue. A company has to, for example, think through the impact of price on volume, competitors' prices, customer preferences, cost situation, inflation, exchange rates, regulations, and reductions.

To reach their goal (market share, revenue and so on) a company has several pricing strategies to choose from, the four most important strategies are the market-penetration strategy, the market-skimming strategy, the comparable pricing strategy, and the flanking strategy. In *the market-penetration strategy* a company gains an important market share via low prices. Secondly, there is *the market-skimming strategy*. This strategy is used when a company is the first to enter the market, and therefore does not have any competition. To cash in on the actual market opportunities and to compensate for development costs, a high price will be set on the market. When competition enters the market and prices drop, the price setting will be adjusted. In *the comparable pricing strategy*, a company sets the prices on the similar level as the competition and competes using other features – not the price (for example benefits) Lastly, many companies will not only focus on one product, but will try to enter the market with a range of products - product lines- at different prices to reach different target segments. This strategy is called *the flanking strategy*. It creates a net that catches in its system as many customers as possible. (16, 17, 20)

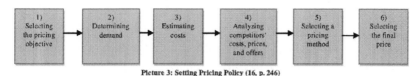

Picture 3: Setting Pricing Policy (16, p. 246)

Despite the fact that a company plans to charge a specific price the customer usually pays less due to price reductions that are very common today. Buyers today more and more expect discounts, free service, or a gift. It is clear that these customer benefits take their toll on the margins on the selling price. Therefore, companies have to have this discounting under control. For this, they can use the following methods:

- **Cost-based pricing** – companies add, as Kotler says, a "markup" to their estimated costs, which ensures that at the end the price covers total costs, and still results in attractive profit margin;
- **Value-based pricing** - companies estimate the highest price that the buyer would pay for the offering and then price their product a little bit under this estimated price. This pricing is based on the perceived value to the customer rather than on the actual costs of the product, the market price, competitors' prices, or the historical price. The only condition to be met is that the costs must be much lower than the value price for and attractive profit;
- **Competition-based pricing** – companies set a price on a similar level as their competition if they expect demand to grow. (17, 20)

In the international environment, it is very difficult to adopt a standardized pricing strategy because of big differences in transportation costs, exchange rates, competition, market demand, strategic objectives, tax policies, legal regulations, distribution channels, and global buyers. Companies usually create a **global pricing strategy** based on flexibility. Their local managers, as they know the best price for their regions, have the possibility to adjust the price within an acceptable range defined by management. To minimize the impact of such adjustments on the entire company, the management can either adopt a pricing policy, when each customer absorbs the extra costs of freight and import duties or they can charge company's various branches. (20, 25)

PLACE (DISTRIBUTION)

Distribution is a way to make the offering available to the target market. It includes distribution channels, locations, inventory, transport, assortments and other. A company can sell the products directly to the end customers (e.g. Avon, Oriflame, Mary Kay, Dell computers), or sell the products through middlemen who sells to the end customers (e.g. Max Factor, Hewlett-Packard), or use both ways. There are many ways how to distribute an offering. The basic ways of distribution and listed below:

- Direct selling (sales agents);
- party selling (sales agent sells to friends);

- multilevel marketing (many independent distributors and channels with multiple level of compensation);
- telemarketing (selling over phone, via internet);
- retailers (selling via other partners);
- dual distribution (usage of both direct selling and retailer selling). (16, 17)

Today there are many different channels of distribution, which allow customer to choose the way in which he wants to do his shopping and where. As most of the people are busy, under time pressure and therefore do not have time to go to a shop, the shopping from home is becoming more and more popular. There are two main options of how to do the shopping:

- **Store-based shopping** is buying from large or small retailer usually for a higher price plus the customer has to drive there, park, stand in line in a store and do other things he might not like;
- **home-based shopping** is buying products offered in catalogs, direct mails, newspapers, magazines, on TV or radio, on telemarketing calls or on the internet usually for lower prices and with the comfort of staying at home. (17)

When deciding on an international marketing strategy, decisions on **international channels** need to be made as well. A company can use two types of international channel alternatives – domestic middlemen who provide marketing services from their local base, or foreign middlemen:

- **Domestic middlemen** are export merchants (carry a full line of manufactured goods), export jobbers (handle mostly raw materials but do not take a physical control of them), trading companies (sell manufactured goods to developing countries and buy back raw material and unprocessed goods), brokers, buying offices, selling groups, and manufacturer's export agents;
- **foreign middlemen** are foreign agents or wholesalers (they shorten the channel and bring the manufacturer closer to the marketplace, but the problem is that they are far away to be controlled properly). (25)

But even after an international company decided on its international channels, chances are big that the company will be faced with a series of problems. The biggest challenge is to establish and maintain effective and efficient distribution network across borders. A company can face various *distribution problems*:

- Needed channel is not available (country allows only state-controlled middlemen, or its economy is not very developed);
- existing distributors have already agreement with other manufacturers;
- control of various channels;
- very costly communicating with the channels (difficult maintaining of interest in manufacturer's product because of the number of middlemen involved). (25)

PROMOTION

Promotion is a communication tool that delivers a message to a target market. It includes five broad areas - advertising, sales promotion, public relations, sales force, and direct marketing which will be discussed in further detail below.

Companies can use two different strategies how to deliver the message. One strategy is *the push strategy*, which is focused on connection and communication between manufacturers and wholesalers or retailers. Manufacturers try to encourage their intermediaries to promote their brand to the customers (give a good shelf space, enable promotions in the stores and so on).

Picture 4: Push Strategy (20, p. 166)

The second strategy is *the pull strategy*. It is focused on connection and communication between manufacturers and the final customers. Manufacturers try to create a brand that is demanded by customer and in this way indirectly influence the intermediaries to offer this brand. Pull strategy usually uses advertising, sales promotion, public relations and direct marketing. (17, 20)

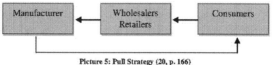

Picture 5: Pull Strategy (20, p. 166)

30

Advertising

Advertising is the most powerful tool for creating awareness of a company, offering, or idea. Advertising is the most efficient when it is narrowly targeted and placed in specific places. Moreover if the add is creative enough it can build image, brand acceptability or even preference of the offering. It the latter case the advertising becomes an investment rather than an expense. Problem remains how a company can measure how much it gets in return for its advertising efforts. (17)

The tool to measure advertising effectiveness is called *return on advertising investment* (ROAI). The difficulty in using this tool lies in the separation of advertising from other communication and marketing mix actions. To calculate the ROAI a company has to evaluate its gross and net sales before and after the advertisement campaign and determine which sales grew as a result of the campaign. That gross sales figure needs to be lowered of the costs of goods or services and divided by the costs of the campaign. A good result of ROAI is a whole number – the larger, the better. If the ROAI is one, the company is at the break-even point. If the ROAI is two, the company got back its investment and also earned a monetary unit for each one spent. (1)

A company that wants to create an advertising can choose the right form of promoting its offering from a broad list of advertisement tools, which includes:

- Print and broadcast ads, reprints of ads;
- packaging – outer, inserts;
- motion pictures;
- brochures, booklets;
- posters, leaflets;
- symbols, logos, directories;
- billboards;
- display signs, point of purchase displays;
- audio-visual material, video DVDs (TV ads have to be very short nowadays which makes it more difficult to tell the message, furthermore it talks to more customers that the targeted ones). (17, 20)

If a company decides to use any type of advertising listed above as a promotional tool it should ensure a high quality of the add. A good and effective advertisement is very complicated to be made but if it is done well it brings profit, creates a high ROAI and can be perceived as an investment. This involves making a lot of strategic decisions on the mission and message of the add, which media to use, how much money to spend and how to measure the benefits the company gains. These features can be summarized into a *five Ms frame* as you can see below:

- Mission (depends on what should the ad create – awareness, interest, desire, or action);
- message (depends on target market and value features);
- media (choice of media through which the message will be communicated);
- money (control of advertising expenditure, based on advertising budget which should deliver the desired reach, frequency, and impact);
- measurement (measuring persuasion scores that increased by brand preference resulting from exposure to the ad campaign). (17)

Sales Promotion

As advertising works mostly on the minds of customers, sales promotion works on the other hand on customers' behavior – it encourages them to act. A customer takes an action after he hears about sales, getting two for the price of one, getting a gift, or a chance to win something. Sales promotions are for companies very costly but help to grow the customer base, attract new customers and bring in "switchers" who are not loyal to any brand. Sales promotion includes:

- Trade promotion (giving retailers special discounts, or gifts);
- consumer promotion (discount - if the differentiation between two offerings is not that obvious, consumer thinks they are equal, then he chooses the one whose price is lower that the list price);
- entertainment, contest, games, sweepstakes, lotteries;
- premiums, gifts;
- demonstration, sampling;
- fairs, trade shows, exhibits;
- coupons, rebates;
- low-interest financing;
- trade-in allowances;

- continuity programs;
- tie-ins. (17, 20)

Public Relations

Companies may use a public relations tool if advertising loses power and sales promotion cost more than was planned for. PR creates and delivers a positive image to the target market. As Kotler says: "Advertising is what you pay for, public relations is what you pray for." (17, p. 111)

Marketing public relations consist of:

- Press kits, publications;
- speeches;
- events, seminars;
- annual reports;
- charitable donations;
- sponsorships;
- community relations;
- lobbying;
- identity media, company magazine.

Apart from the PR tools mentioned above there are also other features that make a big impression on consumers, like: company's stationery, business cards, brochures, factories, offices, trucks, corporate dress code, and uniforms. (17, 20)

Sales Force

Sales force is one of the most expensive marketing communication tools, especially if the sales agents have to operate in the field, travel a lot and spend a lot of time searching for new customers and keeping the existing ones satisfied. However, sales people are more effective than advertising because they have closer connection with customers as they see customers regularly, take them for lunch, entertain them, answer their questions and fix contracts. Sales persons also give valuable feedback to the company about possible improvements of the product, or better value propositions that would be easier to sell. It is called "back-selling". Moreover, the more complex the offering is the more it is necessary to use sales representatives.

Managing sales people is very complex and includes recruiting, selecting, hiring, training, motivation, compensating, and evaluating. There are two tools to improve sales representatives' productivity. One is *time-and-duty analysis*, which shows how the time of a sales person is divided between sales meetings, reporting, selling technique studies, travelling, and customer contact time and helps to adjust it. The other tool for increasing productivity is *sales automation* – usage of laptops, computers, printers, mobile phones, emails, software and so on.

For a company it is important to trace salesperson's costs in relation to the generated sales. This analysis can lead to a more effective sales force, however a company has to be careful that this does no lead to a demoralization (and exodus) of the sales force. Sales persons have to be motivated to sell more and a company should make sure they are well treated and well paid. If they do not feel appreciated enough, they do not sell enough, become frustrated and consequently quit, or are fired and the company has to again recruit and train new people which is very expensive and highly time consuming. Sales force as a tool participates on various actions, which includes:
- Sales presentations;
- sales meetings;
- incentive programs;
- samples;
- fairs and trade shows and other. (17, 20)

Direct Marketing

Today marketers divide market segments into very small groups of customers and realize special offerings for each targeted group separately. The strategy stems from the opportunities provided by specialized media as TV, magazines, and cable networks. Companies create databases where they keep customers profiles in order to define their target markets better, to make special offerings, and to improve their response rates. Direct marketing includes:

- Catalogs;
- mailings;
- telemarketing;
- electronic shopping;
- TV shopping;

- fax mail;
- e-mail;
- voice mail. (17)

1.4.3.2 Product Life Cycle

The previous chapter was about developing the marketing mix strategy (four Ps) before the product is launched. What happens after the launch? As the marketing environment today is very dynamic and product, market, and competitors change over time, the marketing mix has to be flexible as well if a company wants to succeed. The change of the marketing strategy is based on the concept of *Product life cycle*. The product life cycle shows that the product has a limited life and during that life, a lot of features change. It is divided into four stages: Introduction, growth, maturity, and decline. Each stage differs for example in sales, profits, and costs and that is why the marketing objectives and the marketing mix strategy must be adjusted from stage to stage. For more detailed information about the product life cycle see the table number two and the graph number one below. (16, 25)

	INTRODUCTION	GROWTH	MATURITY	DECLINE
CHARACTERISTICS				
Sales	Low	Rapidly rising	Peak	Declining
Costs	High per customer	Average per customer	Low per customer	Low per customer
Profits	Negative	Rising	High	Declining
Customers	Innovators	Early adopters	Middle majority	Laggards
Competitors	Few	Growing number	Stable number beginning to decline	Declining number
MARKETING OBJECTIVES				
	Create a product awareness and trial	Maximize MS	Maximize profit while defending MS	Reduce expenditure and milk the brand
STRATEGIES				
Product	Offer a basic product	Offer product extensions, service, warranty	Diversify brands and items	Phase out weak models
Price	Charge cost-plus	Price to penetrate	Price to match the best market competitors	Cut price
Distribution	Build selective distribution	Build intensive distribution	Build more intensive distribution	Go selective and phase out unprofitable outlets
Advertising	Build product awareness among early adopters and dealers	Build awareness and interest in the mass-market	Stress brand differences and benefits	Reduce to level needed to retain hard-core loyals
Sales Promotion	Use heavy sales promotion to entice trial	Reduce to take advantage of heavy consumer demand	Increase to encourage brand switching	Reduce to minimal level

Table 2: Product Life-Cycle Characteristics, Objectives, and Strategies (16, p. 199)

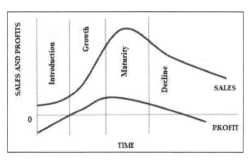

Graph 1: Sales and Profit Life Cycles (2)

1.4.3.3 Marketing Communications Budget

After a company chose all suitable marketing promotion tools for its offering, the way it will be distributed and decided on pricing, it has to estimate all the costs. Every marketing plan must include the estimation of projected marketing costs of launching and selling the product, e.g. salaries of marketing managers, cost of office space. Usually, the biggest part of marketing costs is spent on marketing communication. However, the amount can vary depending on the industry where a company operates. On the one hand, there are companies, which spend thirty to fifty percent of sales on the promotion (e.g. cosmetics industry) and on the other hand, there are companies, which spend only five to ten percent of sales (e.g. industrial equipment industry, business-to-business variations).

To be able to estimate the marketing costs, a company should make a research about the industry, the market, the related competitors and check the internal marketing records to find out which marketing tools were the most successful in the past. Based on this research, the company can take a decision on budget. It can use four basic methods – affordable method, percentage-of-sales method, competitive-parity method and objective-and-task method:

- *Affordable method* (the promotion budget is set on the amount, which management thinks the company can afford);
- *Percentage-of-sales method* (the budget is set at a specified percentage of sales);
- *Competitive-parity method* (the budget is set, lowered or raised based on the actions of competitors);
- *Objective-and-task method* (the budget is set by defining specific objectives, the tasks to achieve them and estimated costs of performing these tasks).

36

After choosing the appropriate method, a company can set the budget. A typical budget consists of salaries for marketing managers, office space, travel costs, personal selling, PR, printing, mailing, brochure design, advertising, networking, sales promotion, event attendance and others. (11, 16)

1.5   IMPLEMENTATION PHASE

When the strategic and tactical plans are defined, it is time to take a decision, based on all information gathered during the planning, whether to implement the marketing plan or not. If the plan is attractive and promises to achieve its objective of making the company competitive in the marketplace, it will be implemented and translated into actions within a time frame.

Implementation starts with obtaining necessary resources, designing marketing organization, and development of schedules. This is followed by the production process, pricing, promotion and distribution. During this phase all the company's departments - R&D, purchasing, manufacturing, sales, marketing, human resource, logistics, finance, and accounting - become active. That is also why at this moment many problems can occur, e.g. it is not possible to produce the product for planned costs, delivered service is worse than it was promised. (17, 25)

1.6   CONTROL PHASE

Every good marketing plan must include a control mechanism tracing and reviewing whether the plan meets its goals. There are two important procedures in controlling the performance of the marketing plan - evaluating and interpreting current results and taking corrective action and auditing marketing effectiveness and developing a plan to improve weak but important components.

The evaluation and interpreting of the results can be done by Benchmarking. The review of benchmarks' performance is measured usually monthly or quarterly as you can see below. If the goals are not reached, the marketing manager must correct and adjust the plan (e.g. some actions, strategies, target market, cancel planned advertising). There is a great variety of things, which can go wrong in a launched marketing program, e.g. wrong target group, wrong price, distribution or communication, or poor implementation. It is very important to find out what exactly went wrong to be able to fix it and above all do it better next time. The best marketing managers learn from their mistakes and that way improve their decision-making for the future. (17, 20)

1.6.1 Current Results – Evaluating, Interpreting and Improving

A company reviews current performance against quarterly or monthly set goals using three different tools – financial scorecards, marketing scorecards, and stakeholder scorecards. These tools help to not only assess the recent situation but also prepare new plans to sustain and improve its future performance.

The financial scorecard is used by company to examine its annual results. It is important to achieve at least the planned value to prove company's strength and to keep the stock price. The financial SC asses performance in sales revenue, costs of goods and others as you can see in the following chart.

The marketing scorecard is used in order to detect any marketing weaknesses that can hide behind good financial results and can in this way help to avoid losing customers. It traces sales growth together with market share growth and assess customers' satisfaction. Management can add also other indicators that are important for a company (e.g. percentage showing cost of salespeople to sales). See the chart below.

FINANCIAL SC	MARKETING SC
Sale revenue	Market growth (units)
Costs of goods	Sales growth
Gross contribution	Market share
Manufacturing overhead	Customer retention
Marketing and sales	New customers
Research and development	Dissatisfied customers
Administrative overhead	Relative product quality
Net profit	Relative service quality
Return on sales (%)	Relative new product sales
Assets	
Assets (% of sales)	
Return of assets (%)	

Table 3: Financial and Marketing Scorecard (17, p. 187-188)

The Stakeholder scorecard (also called Balanced SC) helps to review the level of satisfaction of important stakeholders and company's partners and provides a basis for creating win-win relations. It is not always easy because a company must please not only its stakeholders (employees, suppliers, distributors, dealers and community) but also at the first place its stockholders. To please stockholders a company could pay less to stakeholders but in a long period of time, this could cause loss of good employees, suppliers, and distributors. Therefore, every company has to review and balance its rewards to its various stakeholders. (16, 17, 20)

1.6.2 Marketing Effectiveness Audit

Apart from reviewing the fulfilling of the marketing plan, companies should also periodically examine also its main functions - marketing, finance, purchasing, R&D and others – in a complete, systematic, and independent marketing audit. Auditing marketing effectiveness creates opportunities to improve weak but important components. (16, 17)

AUDITED AREA	AUDITED FEATURES
Marketing Environment	Macroenvironment - Demographic, Economic, Environmental, Technological, Political, Cultural
	Task Environment - Markets, Customers, Competitors, Distribution and Dealers, Suppliers, Facilitators and Marketing Firms, Publics
Marketing Strategy	Business Mission, Marketing Objectives and Goals, Strategy
Marketing Organization	Formal Structure, Functional Efficiency, Interface Efficiency
Marketing Systems	Marketing Information System, Marketing Planning Systems, Marketing Control System, New-Product Development System
Marketing Productivity	Profitability Analysis, Cost-Effectiveness Analysis
Marketing Function	Products, Price, Distribution, Advertising, Sales Promotion, Publicity, Direct Marketing, Sales Force

Table 4: The Components of a Marketing Audit (17, p. 193)

2   COMPANY OVERVIEW

2.1   ST. JUDE MEDICAL, INC.

Founded:	1976
Global Headquarters:	St. Paul, Minnesota, USA
Regional Headquarters:	Asia Pacific (Hong Kong)
	EMEAC[1] (Brussels, Belgium)
	Japan (Tokyo, Japan)
	Latin America (Sao Paolo, Brazil)
	USA (Austin, Texas)
Global Reach:	Products sold in more than 100 countries
Facilities:	More than 20 principal operations and manufacturing facilities worldwide
Employees:	More than 14 000 worldwide
Net Sales:	$4,681 billion in 2009
R&D Investments:	At least 12% of sales per year.
Company Culture:	ISO 14001, AdvaMed Code of Ethics
Brand Promise:	More Control. Less Risk.
Webpage:	www.sjm.com
Stock exchange:	New York Stock Exchange (15)

St. Jude Medical is an American company that develops medical technology and services. They are dedicated to improving the practice of medicine by putting more control into the hands of physicians, reducing risk and contributing to successful results of the treatment. SJM is focused on the treatment of cardiac, neurological and chronic pain diseases worldwide and that is why the four major focus areas include: cardiac rhythm management, atrial fibrillation, cardiovascular and neuromodulation.[2]

---

[1] Europe, Middle East, Africa, Canada.
[2] *Sjm.com* [online]. c2010 [accessed 2011-01-17]. Available on:
< http://www.sjm.com/corporate/about-us.aspx>.

2.2   COMPANY DEVELOPMENT

St. Jude Medical has a long history. It was founded in 1976 in St. Paul in Minnesota, USA, as a pioneering manufacturer of bi-leaflet implantable mechanical heart valves. The company's founder, Manuel Villefana, named the company after the patron saint of hopeless causes, as a gesture of gratefulness after praying to him to help his son survive a life-threatening heart condition. Since the SJM's first major acquisition in 1994 (as can be seen on the picture nb. 6 below), the company has grown rapidly and in little over thirty years since its foundation it has become the today's close runner up and has evolved from producing heart valves into the four major focus areas – CRM[3], AF[4], cardiovascular and neuromodulation.

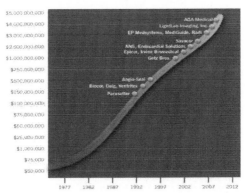

Picture 6: Company Growth and Corporate Acquisition History[5]

In 2010, St. Jude Medical was named by FORTUNE magazine to the FORTUNE 500[6] and has been recognized as one of America's Most Admired Companies for six consecutive years. The company's growth is also visible on the following graphs (nb. 2, 3) that show the net sales and the R&D expenses. We can see that both values are since 2002 gradually growing even despite the global economic crisis. It can be seen however that the crisis slowed down the growth R&D expenses growth follows the net sales growth because of the fact

---

[3] Cardiac Rhythm Management.
[4] Atrial Fibrillation.
[5] *Sjm.com* [online]. c2010 [accessed 2011-01-17]. Available on:
   <http://www.sjm.com/corporate/about-us/history.aspx>.
[6] It is one of the major franchises of the FORTUNE magazine. The annual FORTUNE 500 list ranks all US companies by their revenue.

already mentioned in the first chapter: SJM invests at least 12% of sales per year in the research and development.[7]

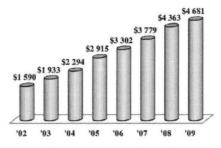

Graph 2: Net Sales (in Millions, 2002-2009) (15)

Graph 3: R & D Expense (in Millions, 2002-2009) (15)

2.3 PRODUCTS

As mentioned in the first chapter, St. Jude Medical has four major focus areas – CRM, AF, cardiovascular and neuromodulation. All activities among these areas are focused on customers' needs. This primary focus drives the search for innovation, quality programs, clinical studies and above all product introductions. The *general product portfolio* includes:

- Implantable cardioverter defibrillators;
- Cardiac resynchronization therapy devices;
- Pacemakers;
- Electrophysiology catheters;
- Mapping and visualization systems;
- Vascular closure devices;

---

[7] *Sjm.com* [online]. c2010 [accessed 2011-01-17]. Available on:
<http://www.sjm.com/corporate/about-us/history.aspx>.

- Heart valve replacement and repair products;
- Spinal cord stimulation and deep brain stimulation devices.[8]

2.4 FOCUS AREAS GROWTH

St. Jude Medical is committed to continuous innovation and growth in its people, product portfolios and clinical research programs. It sees growth opportunities in each of its four focus areas. Below a graph nb. 4 can be found which shows revenue contribution of each area and the recent development of the market. In what follows a short description of AF, CRM, cardiovascular and neuromodulation can be found. The description of AF is more detailed and includes the AF product portfolio as this book is focused on AF products.

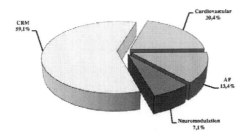

Graph 4: Revenue Contribution by Focus Area (2009) (15)

2.4.1 Atrial Fibrillation

The AF department deals with the illness of ***atrial fibrillation***, which is the most common type of cardiac arrhythmia. It is a problem with the rate or rhythm of the heartbeat. The heartbeat can be too fast (tachycardia), to slow (bradycardia), or with and irregular rhythm. In a healthy heart an electrical signal spreads from the top of the heart to the bottom with each heartbeat and that causes the heart to contract and pump blood as the signal travels. In a heart with an AF problem, the electric pulses are disorganized and that is resulting in an irregular contraction (fibrillation) of the two upper chambers of the heart. Most arrhythmias are harmless, but some can be serious or even life threatening as it can cause the heart being

---

[8] *Sjm.com* [online]. c2010 [accessed 2011-01-18]. Available on:
<http://www.sjm.com/corporate/about-us.aspx>.

unable to pump enough blood to the body. Lack of blood flow can damage the brain, heart, and other organs.[9]

St. Jude Medical is a pioneer and leader in the AF market, which is estimated to be about $2 billion. It offers the industry's broadest product portfolio for the EP[10] lab that helps physicians in the diagnosis and treatment of cardiac arrhythmias. The *AF product portfolio* includes:

- Introducers and Diagnostic Catheters;
- Mapping and Visualization Systems;
- Surgical and Catheter-Based Ablation Devices;
- Recording Systems;
- Implantable Cardiac Monitors. (See appendix nb. 1 for product names and pictures).

SJM is also sponsoring the following clinical researches: IRASE AF (Irrigated Ablation System Evaluation for AF), which could lead to an AF indication for an ablation catheter, and CABANA (Catheter Ablation versus Anti-arrhythmic Drug Therapy for Atrial Fibrillation Trial). Both researches show the company's commitment to advancing the management of AF.[11]

2.4.2 Cardiac Rhythm Management

Cardiac rhythm management department is concerned with a broad field of expertise with the goal of managing "abnormal" heart rhytms. Most wellknown examples of CRM devices are pacemakers (which support the heart in obtaining a steady, constant heart rhythm) and Internal Cardiac Defibrilators (which provide the heart with an internal shock when the heart stopped beating). The CRM department is the biggest contributor to SJM's revenues. The market was approximately $11 billion in 2009. The new CRM devices launched in 2009 include RF[12] pacemakers, an ST segment (Electrical changes between heartbeats) monitoring

[9]. *Nhlbi.nih.gov* [online]. 2009 [accessed 2011-03-12]. Cardiac Heart Arrhythmias. Available on:
   <http://www.nhlbi.nih.gov/health/dci/Diseases/arr/arr_whatis.html>.
[10]Electrophysiology.
[11] *Sjm.com* [online]. c2010 [accessed 2011-01-18]. Available on:
   < http://sjm.com/corporate/about-us/company-fact-sheet.aspx>.
[12] Radio frequency.

ICD[13,] and a cellular adaptor for the Merlin@home™ remote monitoring system. In 2010 SJM has begun clinical trials on a number of new technologies including a left atrial pressure monitor, an MRI[14]-compatible pacemaker and a quadripolar pacing system.[15]

2.4.3 Neuromodulation

The neuromodulation department operates in the field of study where chronicle pain disorders are treated by overpowering the pain impulses with electrical impulses. The electrical impulses (generated by a battery implanted in the body) are delivered straight into the human brain ("deep brain stimulation") or in the Spinal Chord. The market for Neuromodulation devices is growing rapidly because of the technological developments in this area. Furthermore currently scientific research is ongoing to assess the impact of the treatment on diseases like Alzheimer, Parkinson and migraine which could provide a future boost to the NMD[16] market. St. Jude Medical participates in the $1 billion spinal cord stimulator market and the $360 million DBS[17] market. The company launched its first DBS system in Europe during 2009, and has the smallest, longest lasting spinal cord stimulator on the market. The ongoing clinical researches of SJM are focused on potential indications for depression, Parkinson's disease and numerous other disease states.[18]

2.4.4 Cardiovascular

The cardiovascular department focuses on cardiovascular and heart valve diseases. There are two most important categories of the heart valve diseases: Narrowing of the heart valve and a leaky valve. The best-known treatments provided by SJM for these diseases are the placing of a new valve (mechanical heart valve or tissue valves) or a heart valve repair. SJM participates in segments of the interventional cardiology and cardiac surgery markets

---

[13] Implantable Cardioverter Defibrillator.
[14] Magnetic Resonance Imaging.
[15] *Sjm.com* [online]. c2010 [accessed 2011-01-18]. Available on:
< http://sjm.com/corporate/about-us/company-fact-sheet.aspx>.
[16] Neuromodulation.
[17] Deep Brain Stimulation.
[18] *Sjm.com* [online]. c2010 [accessed 2011-01-18]. Available on:
< http://sjm.com/corporate/about-us/company-fact-sheet.aspx>.

approximately \$2,5 billion. In 2010 the company has entered the markets for pericardial stented tissue valves and coronary guide wires with the launch of Trifecta™ and Roll-x™.[19]

2.5 COMPANY STRUCTURE

SJM is a global company, which is operating in more than hundred countries all over the world. The corporate headquarters is in St. Paul, USA, and controls regional headquarters (see the chart below). The regional headquarters take decisions within the regions that belong to them with the approval from the corporate headquarters for matters that influence the entire company. To make the company structure complete, it includes also eight manufacturing plants in the USA (Arizona, California, Minnesota, New Jersey, Oregon, Puerto Rico, South Carolina, Texas) and six international manufacturing plants (Brazil, Israel, Malaysia, Sweden, Thailand, Costa Rica). (See appendix nb. 2)

CORPORATE HEADQUARTERS	
St. Paul, Minnesota, US	
Regional Headquarters	Geographic Division
Hong Kong	Asia Pacific
Brussels, Belgium	EMEAC
Tokyo, Japan	Japan
Austin, Texas, US	United States

Table 5: Overview of SJM structure

For the purpose of this book, only the regional headquarters in Brussels in Belgium, which controls geographic division EMEAC will be described in more detail.

The geographic division EMEAC contains many countries and that is why it needs to be divided into smaller parts. In total there are three zones *EMEAC 1, 2 and 3*.

EMEAC 1 - Northern and Central Europe:
- Austria, Belgium, Denmark, Estonia, Finland, France, Germany, Iceland, Maghreb (Algeria, Libya, Mauritania, Morocco, Tunisia), Netherlands, Norway, Poland, Sweden, Switzerland.

EMEAC 2 - Southern Europe, United Kingdom/Ireland and Canada:
- Canada, Ireland, Italy, Portugal, Spain, United Kingdom.

---

[19] *Sjm.com* [online]. c2010 [accessed 2011-01-18]. Available on:
< http://sjm.com/corporate/about-us/company-fact-sheet.aspx>.

EMEAC 3 - Emerging markets and Distributors:
-   Eastern Europe (Baltic countries, Czech Republic, Hungary, Serbia and others), Israel, Middle East (Lebanon, Saudi Arabia, Turkey and others). (15)

In what follows, the analytical part, the focus will remain on the EMEAC countries, more specifically on the European Union member states.

3   ANALYTICAL PART

The analytical part will familiarize readers with the information about the new product launch that will be needed as a basis for creating the next chapter called The Propositions for Improvements.

This chapter will describe and analyze the process of the creation and implementation of the marketing plan in order to find critical points. Based on the analysis, the next chapter will identify critical points and weak points in the entire procedure and propose improvements to this process.

Before the analytical part starts, it is important to provide some relevant facts and details about the structure of BCC[20], the medical procedure of the cardiac ablation and describe the medical devices to be launched. This will provide readers with some needed background knowledge in order to come to a better understanding of the marketing plan itself.

3.1   STRUCTURE OF BCC

St. Jude Medical is a global company that is divided into smaller sections as it was said in the company overview chapter. The two biggest parts are the US division and the International division. As the US division is not relevant for the book, the focus is on the International division. The ID[21] is further divided into Asia, Japan and EMEAC. This book is focused explicitly on activities of the marketing department in the Brussels Coordination Center. As it is the regional headquarters of EMEAC, it controls product launches only within this area (EMEAC 1, 2, 3 defined in the company overview). For the purpose of the book that is to demonstrate the marketing product launch of medical devices, I decided to focus only on a part of EMEAC, more specifically only on the European Union market and its twenty-seven member states[22] for simplification.

---

[20] Brussels Coordination Center.
[21] International Division.
[22] Austria, Belgium, Bulgaria, Cyprus, Czech Republic, Denmark, Estonia, Finland, France, Germany, Greece, Hungary, Ireland, Italy, Latvia, Lithuania, Luxembourg, Malta, Netherlands, Poland, Portugal, Romania, Slovakia, Slovenia, Spain, Sweden, United Kingdom.

3.2   CARDIAC ABLATION

All people working at the marketing department, especially the managers, have to have a detailed knowledge of the products that they are promoting as well as of the medical procedures the products are intended to be used for. It is not necessary to go into detail for this book but a general explanation is important to come to a better understanding, especially for those readers who have never heard anything about the cardiac ablation before.

In general, the catheter ablation is used to correct the spots in the heart from which the electrical signals causing the heartbeat are sent. If there are too many of these spots, the heart beats irregularly and that results in health problems that have to be cured otherwise they could be life threatening. The physician uses the ablation catheter to burn the extra spots in the heart in order to disable them to send any extra electrical signal in the future. To recognize the spots that have to be ablated the physician uses the mapping system that provides him with a 3D picture of the heart. The more detailed description of the catheter ablation is in the following paragraph.

"Catheter ablation is an invasive procedure used to treat cardiac arrhythmias[23] and is done after a comprehensive electrophysiologic study. The procedures are performed in the EP laboratory where small tubes called catheters are placed into the veins and arteries in the legs, and sometimes arm or neck and passed to the heart. Most ablation catheters use radiofrequency energy to heat its tip. This catheter is placed in the heart near the area causing the arrhythmia and ablates or destroys this abnormal pathway. The key to performing catheter ablation is the mapping of the cardiac arrhythmia, which allows the electrophysiologist to determine where in the heart the arrhythmia arises and consequently determine the location for the placement of the ablation catheter. The complete procedure takes usually up to four hours. The patients are monitored overnight after the procedure and if there are no complications they can go home the next day and return to normal activities in few days."(5)

The book is based on my personal work experience in BCC where I had an internship at the AF marketing department. The next chapters will show the knowledge I gained at SJM and will describe the creation of a marketing launch plan for medical devices, more specifically for the ablation catheters and the mapping systems as parts of the SJM AF portfolio.

---

[23] Heart Beat Irregularities.

3.3 PRODUCTS TO BE LAUNCHED

The book will describe and try to optimize a launch plan of an ablation catheter called the ViewFlex™ PLUS ICE and a mapping system called the ViewMate™ Z Intracardiac Ultrasound Console as these two systems work together.

Ablation Catheter

"The ViewFlex™ PLUS ICE Catheter is a temporary intracardiac ultrasound catheter that is intended to be used to visualize cardiac structures and blood flow within the heart when connected to a mapping system called the ViewMate™ ultrasound console." (See appendix nb. 4) (15)

Mapping System

"The ViewMate™ Z Intracardiac Ultrasound Console is a mapping system that is indicated for use in adult and adolescent pediatric patients to visualize cardiac structures and blood flow within the heart." (See appendix nb. 4) (15)

3.4 CREATION OF A NEW PRODUCT LAUNCH PLAN

Decisions about new products, innovations, company strategy, product strategies and other important issues are taken in the corporate headquarters in St. Paul in US. All SJM products are developed in US as well. Therefore, the product launch procedure usually starts in the US and in a later stage, the product is launched in the SJM international division. However, this can differ from product to product depending on the legal requirements in certain areas. As mentioned before I will describe the product launch only in the EU member states. The starting point of the creation of the marketing plan to launch a new product within the EU are the guidelines received from the global headquarters. The information should contain the time frame that sets a date of the full launch of the product. However, it is on BCC to decide where exactly to launch, which countries to skip - because of the lack of market opportunities - and to manage the entire process.

The person who is creating and managing the marketing plan is a marketing manager – in our case it will be the AF EMEAC marketing manager. Creation of a successful plan is a difficult and a very complex task that requires the manager to have the comprehensive overview and information about the corporate headquarters' instructions, about the new product, competitors, the situation on the market and the company departments' activities. This overview is needed as the launching of a new product not only involves the marketing department but almost all the departments within the company. The departments involved in the launch of the above mentioned products at BCC are the following:

- Clinical;
- Education;
- Field Effectiveness;
- Finance & Administration;
- Human Resource;
- Information Technology;
- Legal, Regulatory, Quality Affairs & Business Development;
- Marketing/Marcom[24];
- Operations/Capital Equipment Service;
- Reimbursement & Health Economics. (15)

Some departments are involved in the creation of the marketing plan if the plan includes tasks for them. Other departments are not included in the plan but are also important for the smooth procedure of marketing and selling medical devices.

The creation of a new product launch plan for an international market has to be based on a detailed analysis of the product itself, of the company and the environment where the company is operating. As the product is launched in an international environment we also have to consider the differences, specifics and details related to particular countries. We have to understand the market because all these information are important and necessary for developing a successful plan and for reasonable decision-making. The analysis of this information will be discussed in the following chapters, e.g. specifics, risks, strategies, segmentation, targeting, SWOT, SLEPT.

---

[24] Marketing Communication. It is a department that creates marketing materials and participates on all product launches.

3.4.1 Starting Point

The impulse for starting the preparation of the marketing plan for EMEAC, in our case for the EU, is an information sent from corporate headquarters to BCC, as mentioned in the previous chapter. At that point, the product is already developed, approved and launched in US and that is why the steps of deciding on research as well as of designing and developing the product are already completed. As the product is already being produced, BCC planning focuses on the product launch. The deadline of the product launch is set by the corporate headquarters but for the rest it is upon the marketing manager to create a plan that could fulfill the US expectations within the given budget.

3.4.2 Analysis Of The Current Situation

Product launch in the European market is easier due to the common rules that are adopted by all EU member states. For this reason, there are specifics (e.g. trade barriers political barriers) which will not be as relevant to the launch plan as other specifics (e.g. language barriers, distribution channels). The specifics, which could have an impact on the smooth product launch, are:

- *Legislation and regulation:* Production and selling of medical devices is governed by common rules within the entire EU but there are some exceptions when the national bodies require more. This will be described in more detail further in the SLEPT analysis as it can cause delays in the launch.
- *Trade barriers:* The trade barriers are erased due to the four freedoms - free movement of goods, capital, services, and people and that makes business of SJM easier.
- *Political barriers and risks:* This includes monetary restrictions (regards both the countries that joined the monetary union and adopted euro and the countries that still have their own currency), strikes, terrorism, natural disasters (floods, fire, earthquake). All this can result in problems that will influence the smooth launch procedure.
- *Country risks:* All EU members are more or less stable thanks to the help of the EU. The risk of the SJM's procedure is low.
- *Commercial risks:* The conditions for business activities of foreign companies can differ in each country and finding reliable business partners can be difficult for the foreign

companies. SJM lowers these risks by receiving the relevant and updated information from the country managers.

- *Social and cultural differences and their influence on behavior and decision of customers:* There is a great variety of differences among the countries of EU and from this reason, the companies have to be watchful not to miss anything. However, selling the medical devices is not as influenced by these social factors as selling e.g. customer goods.

- *Financial risks:* Exchange risks are lowered due to the existence of the Euro zone, however SJM still faces above all the US dollar exchange rate and other European currencies' exchange rates.

- *Survey of new foreign markets:* SJM is already present in almost all EU member states and can use the information from the previous launches and from the managers' experience.

- *Entering distribution channels:* SJM has its own offices or distributors in all EU countries and uses similar channels for all the launches.

- *Language barriers and adaptation of the marketing mix:* Regarding the medical devices, the only adaptation is the translation of marketing materials. This will be described in more detail in the chapter of the Marketing mix.

3.4.2.1 PEST Analysis

In the following chapter, the features of the political, economic, social and technological environment will be described with the help of the PEST analysis.

Political, legal, and regulatory environment

The medical products that we plan to launch have to be approved by the appropriate bodies according to the EU legislation. The conditions can differ depending on the type of a device. Mostly the CE mark is needed to be able to sell the device in the EU. It is the task of the Legal, regulatory, quality affairs & business development department to successfully complete the process of gaining the CE mark. The marketing department is not concerned with this process but has to implement it in the plan because it can take a very long time (from months to years) and without the CE mark, no medical devices can be sold. For the launch of the medical device, the company has to take into account following regulations:

- EU legislation;
- National legislation of the EU members;
- Medical Device Regulations (by World Health Organization) (26);
- The Medical Device Directive (Council Directive 93/42/EEC) amended by the 2007/47/EC (10);
- CE marking (7).

As the process of gaining the CE mark is not owned by the marketing department, we will assume that the new product has the CE mark and is approved by both EU and the national notified bodies.

Economic/Demographic environment

In general, the member states of the EU can be divided into two groups. In the first group, there are countries that are in the Euro zone (Austria, Belgium, Cyprus, Estonia, Finland, France, Germany, Greece, Ireland, Italy, Luxembourg, Malta, Netherlands, Portugal, Slovakia, Slovenia and Spain) and in the second group, there are countries outside the Euro zone (Bulgaria, Czech Republic, Denmark, Hungary, Latvia, Lithuania, Poland, Romania, Sweden and United Kingdom). Doing the business with the countries that adopted Euro is easier because of the common currency, however there are recently three indebted countries of the Euro zone that are undergoing a crisis. This crisis highers the risks on their markets. They are Greece, Portugal and Ireland. SJM has to take into account not only the exchange rates of Euro and other European currencies but also the exchange rate of the US dollar as the headquarters is situated in the US and most of the financial documents are presented in dollars. To avoid problems and to be able to compare all results during the entire year, SJM uses fixed exchange rates determined at the beginning of the year.

Social and Cultural environment

Medical devices are not being sold to the end users but to the doctors and the management of the hospital where the doctor works. The end users (patients) do not care about the medical devices as such that are used to cure them. They are focused on being healthy again, regardless of the brand of the medical device used. For this reason, the values and beliefs of the final users are not for the marketing managers as relevant as the physicians' beliefs. Therefore, it is more important to know the physicians and to be in the contact with the management of the hospital. This is the task of the sales representatives in each country.

They have to know the physicians, their beliefs and values in order to impress them with the offering.

Technological, Competitive and Infrastructure Environment

Medical devices market is a very competitive market and contains only a few strong players. All medical devices producers are investing large amounts of money in research, development and innovations. In this market, the company who brings the innovative technology the first, usually wins or has a considerable competitive advantage.

Competitors of the SJM in the ICE field are BARD, GE, Siemens and Cardiotek. In what follows a basic fact sheet of the different companies will be provided.

BARD

- Founded in 1907.
- 11 000 employees.
- Leading multinational developer, manufacturer and marketer of medical technology.
- Producer of Vascular, Urology, Oncology and Surgical Specialty products.
- Corporate Strategy focused on a Disease State Management.
- Investments in R&D were $179 million in 2009.
- Member of AdvaMed.
- Electrophysiology Division offers diagnostic and therapeutic ablation catheters, computer-based EP mapping and recording systems, temporary pacing electrodes, and vascular/cardiac access devices.
- Product - LabSystem™. (9)

GE Healthcare

- Headquarters is in United Kingdom.
- 46 000 employees.
- It is a $17 billion unit of General Electric Company.
- Produces products to diagnose and treat cancer, heart and neurological diseases.
- $6 billion is committed to continuously develop innovations.
- Operates in Americas, Asia-Pacific, China, EMEA and India.

- Key care areas are Cardiology, Neurology, Emergency Medicine and Oncology.
- They put emphasis on Women's health.
- Product - CardioLab®, Mac-Lab®, ComboLab. (12)

Siemens

- Founded in 1847.
- 405 000 employees.
- R&D investments were €3,9 billion in 2009.
- Operates in Europe, Middle East, Africa, Asia, Australia and Americas.
- Focuses on following businesses – Industry sector, Energy sector, Cross-Sector businesses, Cross Sector Services, Healthcare Sector and Equity Investments.

Siemens Healthcare

- Subdivision of Siemens.
- 48 000 employees.
- Fields of interest are Cardiology, Oncology, Neurology, Women's health, Urology, Surgery and Audiology.
- Business Excellence in Cardiology offers Consulting, Financial Services, Refurbished Systems, Education, Information Systems, IT infrastructure, Services.
- It creates 15% of the total revenue of Siemens.
- Product - Artis zee, Artis zeego. (23)

Cardiotek

- Based in Maastricht in the Netherlands.
- Since 1980 cooperates with the group of Prof. Wellens and Bruga at the University of Maastricht in developing early versions of EP systems.
- First product was a microprocessor based programmable stimulator.
- As the first company developed PC based multi channel intra cardiac amplifier system for clinical mapping during surgery procedures.
- Product - EP-TRACER. (6)

EXTERNAL FACTORS	OPPORTUNITIES	THREATS
Political	- Reimbursement and social health care policies can be subject to change	- Reimbursements by government are subject to changes - Political situations can change (cfr. Belgium) and can cause a threat to the continuity of doing business
Economic	- The Medical device industry is only moderately impacted by the economic crisis - Economical situation has been improving - Medical Device Market is a growing market	- EMEA market is heterogeneous - Different currencies (Euro vs. non-Euro countries) - Economical crisis has indebted three EU countries leading to an increased risk - Exchange rate €/$ impacts margins (US company)
Social	- End customers are not familiar or loyal to brands, good personal relationships with doctors and hospitals will help the gain of market share and sales	- Dependency on personal relationships with doctors and hospitals can provide a risk when relationship deteriorates
Technological	- SJM has a strong reputation concerning High Tech devices and innovative products - SJM is entering the ICE market with a strong and innovative product	- Competitive market - New Innovative Technologies by competitors can provide a risk and loss of market share/sales - Heavy R&D investments are needed but can way on margins
Law	- CE mark was obtained - Products are conform The Medical Device Directive	- National legislation of countries can be divers within EMEA and can change - Medical Device Regulations of the world health organization have to be met at all times

Table 6: Overview of the External Factors

3.4.2.2 SWOT Analysis

Based on the following chart describing the strengths and the weaknesses of the SJM's internal factors and the chart in the previous chapter describing the opportunities and the threats, the SWOT analysis will be made.

The internal factors summarized in the chart below are based on the earlier mentioned chapter called Company overview and also on the chapters further in the book, mainly Marketing mix, where more detailed explanation is provided.

INTERNAL FACTORS	SJM (as a whole)	STRENGTHS of BCC	WEAKNESSES of BCC
Strategy	- Becoming the global leader in the medical device industry by providing physicians with instruments that give them more control thus reducing the risk of procedures and providing better (successful) outcomes to patients over the entire world.	- The vision of the company is clear for all employees throughout BCC and are lived by the employees.	- N/A.
Structure	- SJM has a matrix structure by division (CRM/AF/Neuromodulation/Cardiovascular) and Region (International Division (EMEAC 1-3; Asia pacific; Japan) and US).	- Clear aligned responsibilities and synergies throughout the world (per division) are obtained.	- The divisions within BCC get their instructions from their counterpart in the US and that can cause possible timing and/or communicating issues.
Systems	- Decisions are taken Top down; but taking into account input from local management (bottom up). Final decision is taken by upper management and implemented throughout the organization. To facilitate the process an integrated ERP (SAP) system is used together with Reporting tools (BW and BEX analyzer and Sartac) as well as workflows for approvals. Due to the industry (medical) a close record is kept with key decisions and changes to Quality procedures.	- Central management makes for easy decision making (Top-to-Bottom) - Integrated ERP and Business Intelligence systems provide useful and easy accessible information for decision making.	- Complicated communication with US that has to give an approval to every important decision. - Difficulties because of the time difference (Europe/US). - Due to the (legally required) strict procedure there is a time lapse before changes can be implemented.
Style (of management)	- Adherence to the upper management is expected although there is some room for open communication that can lead to innovative results.	- There is a clear identification of who is upper management and who's lead needs to be followed.	- Due to the great number of offices throughout EMEAC it can be a challenge to align management in all countries.
Staff	- The staff categories within SJM vary from Warehouse handlers over clerks to management and upper management. Structural performance reviews, scorecards and appraisal interviews exists and are mandatory at all levels giving incentive and opportunities to all employees.	- Staff monitoring and coaching are structuralized/obliged and instruments (scorecards, appraisal interviews) are provided to management and employees, giving incentive to staff and providing growing opportunities within the organization which leads to more motivated staff.	- Although monitoring and coaching is obliged this is not always done/not done into depth leading to a higher rate of departures.
Skills	- SJM staff is knowledgeable about the offered products through intensive training. - Due to the strict quality requirements within the medical industry, staff received a thorough quality training throughout the entire organization.	- There is a culture of product training and product understanding supported by a (SJM owned) education center and a wide network of medical professionals. - Trainings are frequent and institutionalized throughout entire BCC and cross-divisional.	- If a new market is entered (cfr ICE market) it can take some time before sales and educational staff is fully trained and experienced in comparison with the competitors and market expectation.
Shared values	- All employees are aware and trained in the "More Control. Less Risk." "doctrine". Reaching this goal through Quality and consistency.	- Values are known and closely monitored and shared throughout the entire organization.	- N/A.

Table 7: Overview of the Internal Factors

58

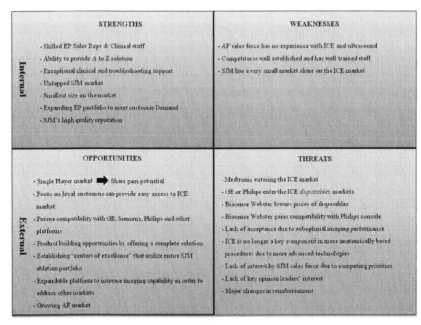

STRENGTHS	WEAKNESSES
- Skilled EP Sales Reps & Clinical staff - Ability to provide A to Z solution - Exceptional clinical and troubleshooting support - Untapped SJM market - Smallest size on the market - Expanding EP portfolio to meet customer Demand - SJM's high quality reputation	- AF sales force has no experience with ICE and ultrasound - Competitor is well established and has well trained staff - SJM has a very small market share on the ICE market
OPPORTUNITIES	THREATS
- Single Player market ➡ Share gain potential - Focus on loyal customers can provide easy access to ICE market - Pursue compatibility with GE, Siemens, Philips and other platforms - Product building opportunities by offering a complete solution - Establishing "centers of excellence" that utilize entire SJM ablation portfolio - Expandable platform to increase imaging capability in order to address other markets - Growing AF market	- Medtronic entering the ICE market - GE or Philips enter the ICE *disposables* markets - Biosense Webster lowers prices of disposables - Biosense Webster gains compatibility with Philips console - Lack of acceptance due to suboptimal imaging performance - ICE is no longer a key component in more anatomically based procedures due to more advanced technologies - Lack of interest by SJM sales force due to competing priorities - Lack of key opinion leaders' interest - Major changes in reimbursement

(Internal / External labels on left side)

Table 8: SWOT Analysis (15)

3.4.2.3 Objectives

No plan can be made before setting a goal to be reached. Knowing the facts from the situational analysis described in the previous chapters allows SJM to assess the starting point and to establish the final goal. Based on this, SJM also determines how to reach the goal, obtain the financial and human resources and position the company to get a sustainable advantage. The marketing goals should be consistent with the ultimate business objectives of the company and contribute to it. The goals of the new product launch plan and the overall business objectives are the following.

The new products launch goals
- Gain a market share of 30% by 2015. (Current global ICE market is approximately $50 million, SJM has currently less than 10%).
- Reach $2 million ICE catheter sales in 2011.

Business objectives

- Establish a foundation for today and future products.

- To be viewed by the customers as an ICE player.

- Demonstrate SJM's commitment to AF.

- Extend SJM's strong EP lab capital offering.

- Support the brand promise "More Control. Less Risk.".

- Gain ability to more effectively meet the needs of the customers with better technology. (15)

3.4.2.4 Segmentation and Targeting

Different market segments are mapped and targeted by the offices in each EU country. Each country manager and product manager knows his sales people and the sales people know their customers in detail. The decision about in which countries to launch the products is taken by BCC but the proposals of the potential customers come from the sales representatives.

The first stage of launching the new product is called the ***Limited market release***. In the LMR[25] phase, each country office chooses one or more physicians and hospitals (Centers of excellence) that can try the product before it is fully available on the market. The number depends on the size of the country. Of course, there has to be a presumption that they will like the product and that he will help with the further promotion (e.g. writes an article about the product, makes a presentation at the meeting, recommends the product to colleagues). The LMR is planned to start in April 2011.

In the second stage, called the ***Full market release***, the product is widely available to the physicians in all the countries where it was launched. The FMR[26] is planned in June 2011 according to the time frame that will be described later in the chapter of Marketing plan.

3.4.2.5 Positioning

The following positioning of the new products puts their benefits and the way they will be introduced on the market together in one apposite sentence.

"The ViewMate-Z System is a new ICE system designed for exceptional, real-time image guidance and visualization of anatomical structures to help clinicians increase

---

[25] Limited Market Release.
[26] Full Market Release.

confidence when performing complex interventional cardiology and electrophysiology procedures." (15)

3.4.2.6 Messaging

A messaging presents the product's benefits in more detail than the positioning. The messaging of the new catheter and the new mapping system consist of four benefits – visualization, ease of use, catheter size and safety. Further the messaging is also divided by stakeholders (see later).

Visualization

- Real-time visualization of cardiac anatomy for streamlined EP and interventional procedures.
- Premium image quality provides clear images of anatomical structures.
- ViewFlex catheter designed for reliable tip stability to obtain high fidelity images.

Ease of use

- Intuitive software that guides the user through the imaging process.
- Presets and soft keys allow clinicians to save and retrieve settings.
- The ViewFlex catheter incorporates the Agilis NXT handle with its simple one-handed control mechanism.

Size of Catheter

- Small console for reduced footprint in lab.
- Complete digital cardiovascular imaging system that delivers high-definition imaging in a compact, easy-to-use package.
- Portable laptop console to optimize vital lab space and allow for less obstructive workflow.

Safety

- Patient interface module designed to isolate the patient from the system to enhance patient safety.

- Automatic system shut down when catheter temperature threshold is reached. (15)

Segment	Key Messages
Physicians	Ease of use
	Crisp clear images allow the ability to see anatomical structures in real-time
	With the faster computing speed, complications can be visualized as they occur and a plan of action can be determined and implemented quickly
	RF immunity of the system allows to see the underlying anatomy during energy delivery
Staff: Nurses and Techs	Ease of use
	Portable system
	One button preset to get to the system parameters needed for each clinician or type of case
	Easy catheter connections to the system, no need for sterile bag
Patient	Clinician is able to better visualize patient actual anatomy and the effects of the treatment in real-time
	Better outcomes with the potential of increased efficacy and shorter procedure time
	No need for anesthesia or increased recovery time

Table 9: Messaging by Stakeholders (15)

3.4.3 Marketing Launch Plan

The integrated marketing launch plan provides a disciplined approach, specifies all marketing activities and activities of other departments that has to be taken into account within a certain time frame. The plan has to lead to fulfilling the marketing goals that are consistent with other business goals.

The time frame of this product launch is set by the moment when BCC is informed by the US about the launch and by the moment of the full market release. The product launch goals and the business objectives are mentioned in the previous chapter called Objectives. The best way for the marketing manager to realize which activities and items need to be done and at what time they need to be done prior the full market release is to start planning from the endpoint to the beginning. That means to start planning from the date of the FMR, which is June 2011, and go backwards in time to the beginning of planning, in November 2010. A clear and useful way to show this is to create a time frame (see the next page) that shows all activities and milestones by departments that participate in the NPL[27] and their deadlines.

---

[27] New Product Launch.

Table 10: Time Frame of the NPL

	Q4 2010		Q1 2011			Q2 2011		
	NOVEMBER	**DECEMBER**	**JANUARY**	**FEBRUARY**	**MARCH**	**APRIL**	**MAY**	**JUNE**
MARKETING	Marketing Plan Preparation	Awareness Plan		NPL Meeting	LMR	Local Launch, FLM		FMR
	Define Collaterals	Validate Collaterals	Collaterals in English			Collaterals translations		
REGULATORY		Check Regulatory Plan			IFU in English		Local IFUs	
LEGAL	Legal Check		Legal Clearance					
OPERATIONS			1st Forecast		2nd Forecast			
	Service Strategy		Service Plan Ready - Units - Spare parts		Service Team Ready - Educated		Units Ready	
							Service Ready	
EDUCATION		BCC Education		Education Meeting - Marketing Education - Champions Education - Customer CV Planned		Local Training	Sales/FTE Certified Education Programme for Customers	

3.4.3.1 Activities of Departments

The activities of the Marketing/marcom, Legal, regulatory, quality affairs & business development, Operations/capital equipment service and the Education department, who participate on the launch of the product and are directly connected to the marketing mix, are described in this chapter. The marketing mix is described later in the book.

Marketing/Marcom

Marketing department has a leading role in the NPL and has to monitor other departments' activities in order not to be late. The time frame on the previous page shows the following activities that have to be completed/accomplished:

Nov 10	Marketing plan preparation
	Define marketing collaterals (all marketing materials) that will be used for the NPL
Dec 10	Create an awareness plan
	Validate the chosen collaterals by US
Jan-Feb 11	Receive collaterals (e.g. the sell sheet, the ad, the catalog page) in English that are created and already in use in US
Feb 11	Set up NPL meeting for marketing managers from the countries of the EU
Mar 11	LMR in chosen centers
Apr 11	Field leadership meeting
	Local launch meetings to specify the sales strategy
Apr-May 11	Get collaterals' translations into other languages
June 11	FMR

Besides these activities, the marketing department has to take care of the following items, however please note that many of them will be described in more detail in the marketing mix chapter:

- Tactical plan;
- commercial strategic plan;
- sales representatives selection;
- customer segmentation (potential customers are of the highest volume);
- clinical/technical info;
- reference centres;
- Objectives and their measurements;
- Pre-launch, choice of LMR centres of excellece;
- FLM[28], FMR.

---

[28] Field Leadership Meeting.

Legal, Regulatory, Quality Affairs & Business Development

This department takes care of all contracts, of their legal clearance and of other legal requirements including CE marking, quality certificates and notifications of national health bodies in specific countries. The time frame sets these activities:

Nov 10	Legal Check
Dec 10	Check of the Regulatory Plan
Jan 11	Legal Clearance of contracts with distributors
Mar 11	Approval of IFU[29] in English
May 11	Approval of local IFUs

Operations/Capital Equipment Service

The operations/capital equipment service department takes care not only of forecasting, planning and ordering units and spare parts (inventory) but also of service and shipment. The tasks for this department set by the time frame are the following:

Nov 10	Create service strategy
Jan 11	The first forecast of the units
	Service plan ready (units, spare parts)
Mar 11	The second forecast of the units
	Service team educated and ready
May 11	Units and service are ready

Education

Education department takes care both of the internal and external education. That means that they have to create two different training programs and implement them. On the one hand, they have to train the sales representatives and the field technical engineers and on the other hand they have to train physicians and provide them with trials of the products. The education concerning the NPL will be done in the Advanced Learning Center within the ID headquarters in Brussels. According to the time frame, these are the deadlines concerning education:

Dec 10	BCC Education
Feb 11	Education Meeting (Marketing and FTE[30] education)
Mar-Apr 11	Local Training in countries of the EU
May 11	Sales/FTE Certified, Education Program for customers ready

---

[29] Instruction for Use.
[30] Field Technical Engineer.

The creation of the internal education and its implementation consists of these steps:

- Assess knowledge gaps with sales force;
- incorporate market needs;
- establish training objectives;
- define training content;
- prepare country trainers;
- implement training;
- train sales force;
- certify sales force and field technical engineers;
- monitor success;
- assess knowledge gaps after training;
- gather feedback from participants and adjust as needed.

3.4.3.2 Marketing Mix

Product

The products that will be launched are described at the beginning of the analytical part of the book in the chapter called "Products to be launched" which can be found above. They are the ViewFlex™ PLUS ICE Catheter and the ViewMate™ Z Intracardiac Ultrasound Console. For more detailed information, please see appendix number four.

As we are launching medical devices, there are no physical differences (e.g. quality, size, and design), availability differences, service or image differences across the countries of the EU. The only adjustment of these products will be the adjustment of the symbolic values, which means that SJM sells the same product in all countries but the language of manuals and the marketing collaterals are different. This fact lowers the additional marketing costs.

Price

SJM holds a position of a strong company with a long tradition and operates on the marketing devices market, which is a very attractive market. Due to only a few but strong competitors on the market, SJM invests a great part of its available resources in research, development, innovations and also in marketing support of the offering.

SJM, as well as other companies producing and selling medical devices, chooses to follow a Differentiation strategy because its medical devices are very high-tech, perceived as unique, better than competitors' products and with an excellent service. SJM is constantly looking for innovations, has strong marketing abilities, product engineering, personnel and a good reputation. This all has an impact and enables SJM to set higher prices.

In case of the ViewFlex™ PLUS ICE Catheter and the ViewMate™ Z Intracardiac Ultrasound Console, SJM will use the Comparable pricing strategy. The prices will be set high but on a similar level as the competitors' prices because the competitors' technology is alike to SJM's technology and their products are already launched and being sold on the market. However, the new SJM's ViewMate Z system differs from the competition due to certain technological features and mainly due to an excellent service. That all allows SJM to get an advantage and reach its goals - to gain a bigger market share and reach a certain point of sales. This strategy is called the Differentiation strategy.

The comparable price will be set on each EU member state's market separately because it is not possible to adopt standardized pricing strategy due to the differences in transportation costs, competition, market demand, tax policies or distribution channels. The pricing is based on flexibility and the country managers have the possibility to adjust the price within an acceptable range defined by BCC. The pricing process consists of following steps:

- *Evaluation of the Price/Value of Product*: Preparation of the pricing market research (mapping of the competitors' prices), conduction of customer interviews (how do the customers evaluate the product), finalization of the price/value map (putting the first two steps together to create a basis for price setting), creation of the demand curve to evaluate price sensitivity to profit, revenue and market share.
- *Setting Pricing Strategy:* Specification of the average sales price across the EU, adjustments of price in countries with the help of country managers, decision on using after sales/service contracts, discount structures and on multiple product offer strategy, pricing strategy and rules for each country, price floors and ranges.
- *Implementing and Tracking the Pricing Strategy*: development of price tracking system together with IT, tracking average sales price at country level.

Place

SJM sells the products via its offices in the countries or via distributors in case there is no office in the country. However, the medical devices are always being sold through personal selling. The sales representatives who sell devices to physicians have to have excellent marketing skills, have to understand the products and the medical procedures. Therefore, they are continuously educated by SJM in its Advanced Learning Centers.

Selling via SJM Offices:	Austria, Belgium, Denmark, Finland, France, Germany, Italy, Netherlands, Poland, Portugal, Spain, Sweden, United Kingdom.
Selling via Distributors:	Bulgaria, Cyprus, Czech Republic, Estonia, Greece, Hungary, Ireland, Latvia, Lithuania, Luxembourg, Malta, Romania, Slovakia, Slovenia.

Sales representatives' readiness consists of following steps:

- *Development of the Methodology and the Sales Strategy*: Choice of sales representatives, development of training programs for customer service and distribution, sales operation methodology.
- *Targeting Plan*: Definition of criteria for segments, top customer segmentation, determination of metrics (see the chapter "Implementation and control" for more detail), country roll-out plan, sales representatives roll-out plan.
- *Creation and Implementation of the Plan*: Communication of the plan, reached success and problems is crucial.

Promotion

The promotion of medical devices costs a lot of money and is more personal in comparison to other companies producing for example consumers' goods. It is not focused primarily on the end users, although SJM operates a webpage for patients, but on physicians, hospital staff and management. Promotion consists of marketing materials, sales promotion, public relations, sales force and direct marketing.

Marketing Materials

There is a wide choice of marketing materials that can be used at every launch. For the particular launch of these medical devices, SJM will use following collaterals:

- Customer PowerPoint – offers technical and clinical information for customers.
- Sales Training PowerPoint – provides sales representatives with sales training support. It is an internal material.
- Press Release – announcement of gaining the CE mark and of launching the devices.
- Quick Setup Guide – step by step setup guide for customers.
- Catalog page – contains product technical specifications.

68

- System and Catheter Brochure – contains update content and images. (See appendix nb. 4)
- Sell sheet – highlights key messages for the SJM ICE solution. (See appendix nb. 5)
- Ad – creates SJM ICE awareness. (See appendix nb. 6)
- Animation – shows product animation and updated ultrasound images.
- Spec Sheet – summarizes product technical specifications. (See appendix nb. 7)
- Key opinion leader presentation – presentation of a key physician on the new product.
- White paper
- Evaluation form – physician's evaluation of the performance of the particular product. (See appendix nb. 8)
- Web page www.sjmprofessional.com – information for physicians.

Sales Promotion

Sales promotion is a very significant part of promotion while selling medical devices. All medical companies, including SJM, are aware of the fact that they need to have physicians on their side to be successful. There is a wide choice of advantages that the company can offer to the physician in return for his encouragement and goodwill for the new product. Among sales promotion, we can find:

- LMR – chosen physician at chosen hospitals have the opportunity to use the new technology as the first physicians in the EU.
- Field leadership meeting – big launch meeting of SJM management, country managers, AF marketing managers, product managers, sales representatives, AF marketing managers from US and chosen physicians to present the new technology in public before the FMR. It is comprised of workshops, presentations, trials and takes usually at least two days.
- Gifts – any gifts including DVD from tradeshows, PowerPoint presentations and other multimedia.
- Discounts – very rare, only for the top customers.
- Advanced Learning Center – this is a SJM center in Brussels, both for internal and external education, workshops, presentations and any smaller meetings.
- Trade shows – SJM participates at every big congress and trade show to present the products.

Public Relations

- Web page www.health.sjm.com – information and answers for patients.
- Publications.
- Annual reports.
- Sponsorships – charitable contributions.
- Professional education program.
- St. Jude Medical Foundation.

Sales Force

The Sales force is a very expensive marketing communication tool, but it is necessary if the offered product is complex, as for example medical products are. Facts about sales force and their education were already mentioned in the previous chapters. In combination with the above mentioned, the sales force also includes these tools:

- Sales presentations – to teach sales representatives how to sell the product.
- Sales meetings – to teach sales representatives how to deal with physicians.
- Samples – sales representatives show the product to the physicians.
- Fairs and trade shows – offer to the physicians an opportunity of workshop to try to work with the product on a model of a human body.

Direct Marketing

The sales representatives try to keep in contact with the physicians they made a deal with. They inform physician about the new in the industry and offers them participation on new product launches. Direct marketing of SJM includes the already mentioned:

- SJM webpage for professionals.
- SJM webpage for patients.
- Mailings.

3.4.3.3   Medical Device Life Cycle

Product lifecycle management of medical devices is a complicated issue. It is difficult to ensure sustainable revenue growth and market share gains. This field requires from companies not only continuous product innovation, having sufficient available resources, talented and

70

experienced employees but also a having a well balanced product portfolio. The balanced medical devices portfolio has to be ensured by the key marketing leader. The key marketing leader of SJM is the AF Marketing Director who works in the headquarters in US. He should always be focused on customers, understand their needs and wants and consistently propose designing of new products that respond to them. He should also trace the already launched products and map in which stage of the life cycle they are. (19)

The product life cycle has four stages – the introduction, growth, maturity and the decline. The subject of this book is what predates the first stage of introduction and that will take about 8 months according to the time frame. At that moment, although the life cycle has not started yet there is already a certain product awareness created among the physicians and competitors because the system is already launched in US and it has undergone the CE marking procedure in Europe.

In general, the length of the life cycle of a medical device can differ depending on the used technology, the situation on the market and on the competition. Based on the current market information and on the presumptive market development in the future, the life cycle of the ViewMate Z system is estimated to last approximately five to six years.

3.4.3.4 NPL Budget

The budget is set by headquarters in US and it is a task of the AF Marketing Director to keep within this budget. He divides the tasks to other departments (e.g. education, marketing) and sets budget for their activities. The budget that is set for the marketing department can vary depending on the launched product. However, the marketing manager has to trace all marketing activities (e.g. Field leadership meeting) in order not to exceed this budget and ensure cost cutting where possible.

3.4.4 Implementation and Control Phase

The implementation of the new product launch is a complex matter that has to be monitored by the responsible marketing manager. It is important to check if the reality meets the marketing plan and if not evaluate and interpret the differences and take corrective actions. All the results, both positive and negative, have to be communicated to the rest of the marketing team. The key element of tracing the success of the plan is to choose which characteristics will be measured, how and with which kinds of metrics. SJM can determine for example these performance metrics:

- Account targets and plans;
- sales performance;
- inventory management performance
- inventory management versus plan;
- execution of pricing strategy;
- sales representatives' productivity;
- field performance;
- supply chain performance.

The metrics can be measured by various tools but mostly companies use some kind of balanced scorecards. The balanced scorecard measures the performance of chosen items and provides the key stakeholders with updated information of the process.

Besides the balanced scorecard, SJM uses also an evaluation form for physicians assessing the performance of the catheter mentioned already in the marketing mix. (See appendix nb. 8)

This chapter closes the analytical part of the book. The analytical part maps and describes the creation of the ViewMate Z system launch plan and provides the reader with important facts that are necessary for understanding the next part. The next – proposal – part will be based on the analytical part and will look for the critical points, analyze them and propose improvements of the weak points in order to optimize this entire process.

4 STRATEGY PROPOSAL

The last chapter of the book will summarize all facts mentioned in the analytical part and based on this extrapolate the critical and weak points of the procedure as well as propose improvements that would optimize the entire process of the new product launch.

The analytical part describes the process of the product launch of the two new products of St. Jude Medical – the ViewFlex™ PLUS ICE ablation catheter and the ViewMate™ Z Intracardiac Ultrasound Console – that we can simply call the ViewMate Z system. Although SJM launches about forty new products per year within the entire EMEAC, not all launches are the same. Most launches have a lot in common but the importance of the product or system being launched makes for a difference in approach and marketing plan. If it is considered not a very important launch, the marketing budget is very limited. Due to the lack of money, the promotion comprises only of the basic tools creating satisfactory awareness and leaves out the big meetings such as field leadership meeting. In case of the ViewMate Z system launch process that was described in the previous chapter, the importance is very high and the success of the launch is essential for further development and welfare of SJM on the EP market. For this reason, it is necessary to optimize the launch process in order to lower or avoid all possible risks that could cause bad results or failure. These kinds of results would have a negative and long-lasting impact on the SJM's position on the market and could cause a loss of money and a deterioration of the good name of SJM, the employees' motivation and physicians' trust.

Based on the previous paragraph, the overview of the critical points and the proposal of their improvements for the new product launch can be helpful as it can not only avoid the failure of the process but also improve it and help SJM to be in the lead of the competitors.

4.1 CRITICAL POINTS

The product launch includes a lot of key-moments and activities that are crucial for the smooth procedure but might go wrong if they are not taken care of. In this chapter, the reader can find a list of critical activities divided by departments. The departments are Marketing/Marcom, Education, Clinical, Legal, Regulatory, Quality Affairs & Business Development and Operations/Capital Equipment Service. Some of the critical activities are well ensured by the particular department but some of them should be ensured in a better way.

Those activities that need to be improved are a subject of the following chapter called Propositions for Improvement.

4.1.1 Marketing/Marcom

The critical activities within the Marketing/Marcom department were found among the tasks for which the marketing management, marketing and marketing communication are responsible.

4.1.1.1 Marketing Management

- *Managing Employees*: It is difficult to manage employees in such a big company as SJM. The structure of a company is very complex and contains a lot of positions and links. It can be difficult and not clear for some employees to know to who they should refer with diverse issues.

- *Communication with the Headquarters in US*: All important decisions cannot be made without the approval of the headquarters in US. This may cause multiple problems. It can cause delays of projects due to waiting for the orders, cancellations of already well prepared meetings due to cost cutting and communication misunderstandings. Last but not least all the activities are influenced by the time difference. There is a time difference of 7 hours between Minnesota and Brussels implying that most employees in Brussels are almost going home from work when the US employees are only entering their offices. As US is the headquarters, it is the BCC who has to adapt and work longer hours to be able to consult important matters.

- *US Perception of the European Market*: SJM is an American company. Many American companies, SJM included, perceive European market as the American market. They think it is one market and do not take into consideration that only the EU already consists of twenty-seven different nations. These nations have different cultural and social background that influences their decision making. For this reason US headquarters sometimes may not understand the issues BCC is confronted with.

4.1.1.2 Marketing

- ***Project Leader:*** It is necessary to appoint only one project leader that will ensure the smooth continuance of the process. In case of the discussed NPL, the project leader is the AF marketing manager. He divides tasks, tracks the activities and controls keeping the deadlines and the marketing budget. Having only one operator avoids double orders and enables management to get quickly answers and important information about the launch procedure.

- ***Setting Goals:*** To set goals that will motivate and challenge the employees to work better is very important. The question is how to set the goals. They should not be too low but also not too high in order not to lower employees' motivation. In general, the goals should be "smart" – specific, measurable, achievable, realistic and time framed.

- ***Definition of the Communication Strategy:*** The communication strategy is defined at the beginning of the NPL and contains meetings planning (BCC meetings, kick-off meeting, FLM) and choice of the relevant marketing materials. Both issues have to be discussed with the US.

- ***Motivation of Sales Representatives:*** As was said already in the analytical part, the medical devices of SJM are sold through personal selling. This approach requires high quality work of the sales representatives. They have to be well motivated to excel in selling the products. The task of drawing their attention and interest belongs to the tasks of the marketing manager, because the sales representatives are the ones who directly influence the revenues of SJM.

- ***Tracking and Communicating the Success:*** The previous point says that it is necessary to have motivated sales representatives, but this can be extrapolated to all other employees. The entire team that cooperates should be willing to reach better and better results. For this reason, the tracking and communicating of the success or non-success is essential. All team members should be aware of in which stage the launch is and how good were the previous stages. The marketing manager is the one who chooses the tracking method and communicates the success.

- ***Pricing Expectation of the AF Division:*** Pricing in the international environment is a very complex task that is dependant not only on the situation on the market and on the product technology but also on the AF division's expectation.

- ***Choice of the LMR Centers:*** The important task of each sales representative is to appoint suitable physicians and hospital to become a limited market release center. Even more important task of the country managers and the AF marketing manager to decide which

75

appeared centers will be the most interesting ones for the NPL and will support the new product.

4.1.1.3 Marcom

- *Creating the Marketing Materials:* After AF marketing department and the US agree on choice of the marketing materials for a particular launch, the Marcom is in charge of creating them. They follow the instructions, create few proposals and consult them with the marketing manager. Sometimes the instructions are not very clear and that can cause delays in creating the materials.
- *Ordering the Materials:* The Marcom is also responsible for mapping the quality and prices of marketing materials and for ordering them. In case of a wrong order or, for example, order of hundreds of sales sheets with a grammatical mistake, SJM loses a lot of money.
- *Participation on Organizing Meetings:* Marcom helps organizing important meetings by reserving hotels, transportation, ordering marketing materials, contacting audio/visual companies and other.

4.1.2 Education

The activities of the Education department consist of two big parts – an external and an internal education. A type and a level of the training required for a particular launch depends on the importance of the launched device. The chosen education level has to be approved by US. Both external and internal education takes place in the Advanced learning center in Brussels.

- *Internal Education:* This is an education of the internal employees of SJM that is prior to the external education. It comprises not only of the intensive knowledge of the products and the therapy but also of the marketing skills training. It is crucial for SJM to have experienced employees that are continuously developing their skills and knowledge. The training has to be well made otherwise it can cause lack of interest by the Sales Reps or misinformation of the customers by the Sales Reps.
- *External Education:* It is an education for customers that should create a certain awareness of the product. The training provides physicians with the basic information of the products and also with an opportunity to test the product.

4.1.3 Clinical

Clinical takes a lot of time and may cause delays in obtaining the CE mark. Due to the, the entire product launch may be delayed. For example, it is required to observe thirty patients with implanted pacemaker for three month. At first glance it may seem that this stage may be completed after three months, but the marketing manager must not forget to incorporate the time it takes to implant the device. In this case, the implanting would take approximately one month so the entire procedure would last at least four months.

4.1.4 Legal, Regulatory, Quality Affairs & Business Development

The critical activities regarding the product launch of the new ViewMate Z system are also within the Legal, Regulatory, Quality Affairs & Business Development department, more specifically within the Legal and Regulatory unit.

4.1.4.1 Legal

- *Legal Check of Contracts:* Legal unit has an important task to check the legal requirements of all the contracts that SJM fixes with all distributors and suppliers. It is crucial to secure the contracts as they can be fixed for many years and can include certain exclusivity.

4.1.4.2 Regulatory

- *Instruction for Use:* Instructions for use (or IFU for short) are the documents that are delivered together with the products to the customer. The IFU's are a legal requirement and have to be translated into the official language(s) of the country/region. The translation is outsourced and it may take a relatively long time before they are finished and the quality of the translation may differ dramatically. Furthermore, there are countries that have specific regulations that need to be taken into account (for example translations for IFU's in the medical industry in Poland need to be done by government appointed translators).

Secondly, the Instructions for use are often large sized documents, describing the product into great detail. This may appear to be customer unfriendly and a to vast amount of information to go through for a physician every time he/she uses the product.

- *CE Marking:* The CE marking is a crucial step in the launching of the product in Europe. Without the CE certification, a product cannot be launched within EU (and countries outside EU that have adopted the EU standards). However the procedure to get the CE marking appointed is labor intensive and time consuming: the different clinical steps can take up to one year, the timing of gaining the CE marks based on the clinical completion can differ but may also take up to one year.

4.1.5 Operations/Capital Equipment Service

This department is responsible for ensuring the smooth way of products shipment to and from BCC. It also takes care of a service in case of products' defects.

4.1.5.1 Operations

- *Forecasting (units, spare parts):* The Forecasting of the products (Inventory levels needed to support the launch, spare parts to be always on stock or made to order, identification of the critical spare parts) is a difficult exercise for a new product as it cannot be based on historical information but solely on market expectancies (marketing forecasts). Therefore this is a cross departmental exercise between marketing (provide realistic forecasts), inventory management (have efficient stock target levels, reduce storing and transportation costs, meet specific storage and transportation needs concerning for example temperature etc.) and the technical department (identify spare parts and crucial spare parts). A too high stock level will lead to cost inefficient warehousing and transportation, a too low stock level may lead to customer dissatisfaction and potential loss in sales (backorder situations, customer may refer to the competitors products).
- *Transportation and Storage:* Medical devices may require special needs for transportation and/or storage, for example some products have to be stored within a certain temperature range (e.g. above 0 degrees and under 40 degrees) or have to be stored with regards to humidity. It is the operations' responsibility to provide in the needed accommodation and that they are handled with special care when needed.
- The process of transportation should as well take into account that the deliveries can get stuck or delayed at customs, resulting in an increased lead-time from the manufacturing plant.

4.1.5.2 Service

- *Definition of Service Plan:* Medical devices, as for example the ViewMate Z, are complex and regular maintenance and intervention (broken parts) is required. To meet the standards demanded by the customers a strict and clear service plan needs to be enrolled stating who is responsible. These Service Level Agreements are both internally (within SJM) and externally (with the customer, e.g. the time period for a SJM field technical engineer to arrive at the customer location after an incident).

- *Service Time:* Long service times can be a risk in the medical industry. The goal is to avoid incidents through high quality products but, as incidents do happen, to reduce lead-times for intervention as much as possible.

- *Point of Contact:* It is important to establish a clear communication to your customer who they are to contact in case of a defect/issue (establish a Single Point of Contact for the customer).

- *Externally Purchased Products:* Not all components are always produced by SJM but it can happen that some parts are products purchased by SJM from a partner company. Clear rules need to be established what happens with defects to these parts: should they be returned to SJM (BCC or country office?) or directly to the third party producer. Agreements with the third party need to be made on who will be providing in the service costs involved for third party's parts.

4.2 PROPOSITIONS

Managing Employees and Communication

SJM is a vast company with a great number of employees. Communication and finding the correct contact persons is a constant challenge throughout the organization, even more so during a NPL. The communication can be made more efficient and direct by installing clear SPOC's[31] (Single Point of Contacts) per area of interest / area of the NPL. This person(s) manage the communication flows and forward the content to the relevant persons. For the persons communicating, it is at all time clear who to address. This will help to pass on information more efficiently and to all (and only to those) interested parties. Secondly, a "company Wikipedia" can be installed. This "company Wikipedia" would consist of

---

[31] Single Point of Contact.

"articles" about the products, launch, launch schedule and is open to anyone involved in the NPL. This way communication is available for everybody at any time (without involving other parties) and involvement of employees is higher. This could also help change the communication culture within the company and lift it to a higher, more efficient manner.

Creating Problem Awareness Campaign

Most Marketing campaigns primarily focus on creating an awareness of the product. However important this is, emphasis should also be put on the possible problems that can be cured through use of the presented products. This can result in expanding the global size of the market and exceptionally open different markets (markets for which the product was not developed but where the product may offer an alternative solution). This awareness can be created through a forum or discussion groups with both customers (physicians/hospitals), marketing, sales force and product specialists. This can lead to a product "pull" (create the product the customer wants by knowing the customer needs in detail).

Internal Delays in NPL

Internal delays are often caused by the time difference and the difference in priority between BCC and the US division: decisions are taken late, deadlines are not always met although clear milestones are communicated, meetings and projects are cancelled last minute causing big cancelation fees, loss of money and credibility. These problems can be met by installing the BCC management with more (independent) decision power. Secondly, involvement of the US division can be raised by having more US employees full time involved in the BCC launch

Marketing Collaterals

There are many marketing collaterals that SJM can use for the product launch but for the particular launch some collaterals are more relevant than others. To make this clear splitting the products into different groups could help. The products could be divided into three groups according to the launched product – the important NPL, key NPL and a commodity NPL. Each group would have its own relevant materials. Moreover, the Marcom would get assessment from sales representatives that would identify the most powerful collaterals

IFU

There are two problems with the instruction for use. Firstly, the translations from English to other European languages are often delayed. Partially because the English version from US arrives late but also because the translations, which are outsourced by SJM, can differ in quality and are not always reliable. Secondly, the IFU is a large document that can seem to be not clear or confusing.

The solution of the first problem could be provide the US with a clear understanding what such a delay results into and try to make them to give the IFUs a higher importance. This can be done through inviting key-persons in the US to participate with a product launch in the EU. A second improvement initiative can be the creation of a stricter contract with the translators that would be in favor of SJM in case of delays. The solution for the second problem could be to create another document that is smaller and provides customers only with the essential information. It should help the customers to orientate themselves in the complete version.

Operations

When products are ordered in the manufacturing plant, there can be delays in the transportation (e.g. customs) and there can be manufacturing issues leading to the US taking the vast majority of the stock, which can lead to backorders in the International Division. Solution could be to higher stock target levels in the International division, but this brings a considerable additional storage and transportation cost. A more structural solution can be to create an awareness in the US division of the related problems. This could help to reach a more objective distribution of the products (quantity of products put to the disposal per region), for example a distribution based on the sales figures per region. The awareness in the US can be augmented by involving US key persons fulltime in product launches.

Service

In case of a product defect, the customer contacts SJM service and expects a quick solution of the problem. Unfortunately, the time to fix the product defect is too long. To resolve this, SJM could try to resolve issues via software if possible, or ship a new unit in case of cheaper (non-capital) product and hire more field technical engineers to take care of service of more expensive products. A less cost-intensive solution can be the creation of clear SPOC for the customer where they can address their questions and are helped more directly.

FACTOR	ISSUE	IMPROVEMENT
Managing employees and communication	Large enterprise, difficult to identify correct communication channels and contact persons	Establish clear SPOC's per area of the launch to manage communication flow more efficiently
		Establish "Company Wikipedia": information is readily available at any time, raises employee involvement
Awareness campaign	More powerful through problem awareness	Establish a problem awareness (compatible with product awareness) through forums with physicians, marketing, sales and product specialists
Internal Delays	Last minute cancellations by US, missing of deadlines	Install BCC management with more (independent) decision power More full time involvement of US employees
Marketing collaterals	Choice of collaterals	Define three groups of launched products – important, key, commodity
IFU	Translation Delays	Agreement with US/US key-persons participate in launch, better contract with translators created by Legal department
	Big size	Create two versions – complete IFU and smaller version quick steps
Operations	Not enough or too much stock	Involve US key person (fulltime) to reach a distribution based on sales figures per region
Service	Product defect, long service time	Resolve issues via software or shipping out a new unit, have enough available field technical engineers. Clear communication of SPOC

Table 11: Issue/Improvement Overview

	2011							2012
	JUNE	JULY	AUGUST	SEPTEMBER	OCTOBER	NOVEMBER	DECEMBER	
SPOC	Interviews to Establish Precost Flow	Process Analysis	Identification of Areas and Key Persons per Area	Establish Person(s) who become the SPOC				
WIKIPEDIA	Collection of Information about Products and Previous Launches		Analysis of the Data	Identification of Key Areas of Interest	Writing Basic Wikipedia Articles with Information	Further Elaboration of the Site by All involved Employee		
AWARENESS CAMPAIGN		Identification of Possible Candidates to Participate		Contacting Candidates to Find out Their Interest, Identification of Potential Gains	Proposition of Meeting Schedule	Ensuring Each Meeting (Place, Transport, Catering, Accomodation)	Assessment of Meetings, Forwarding Useful Information to Management	
MARKETING COLLATERALS	Collection of Information about Products and Previous Launches		Data Analysis, Creation of the List, Cleansing of the Obsolete Mat.	Splitting Mktg Mat. into Groups, Creation of the Questionnaire	Identification of the Most Effective Mat. in Each Group with the Help of Sales Reps	Creation of Updated List of the Most Effective Mat. According to 3 Launch Groups		

Table 12: The Timeline of the Propositions (SPOC, Wikipedia, Awareness Campaign, Marketing Collaterals)

83

4.3 FORECASTED COSTS AND GAINS

Managing Employees and Communication

Based on the estimation of working hours spent on creating SPOC, which is fifty hours, and on the average wage of sixty dollars per hour, the forecasted costs of establishing SPOC are three thousand dollars. Once the SPOC is established, the costs consist of part of the wage equal to the time of the employee(s) spent on managing the communication flows as the SPOC. The forecasted costs of creating basic Wikipedia are six thousand dollars. The employees would spend creating the site approximately hundred hours. Later the costs of writing articles are very low.

The implementation of both proposed projects would improve the overall communication in the BCC. The increased efficiency of communication saves time, improves the quality of life and work for the employees of BCC and lowers the risk of delays of NPL but it will take some time before the employees get used to use the SPOC and the Wikipedia. The gains will be achieved by more effective communication, avoiding cancellation fees and time saving.

Creating Problem Awareness Campaign

The projected costs depend on the number of planned meetings and on the number of participants. Meetings can be integrated in already planned meetings leading to minimal costs. The estimated costs are based on the plan of meetings that will take place during congresses next year and a half.

The gains are estimated according to the advantage SJM gets as they will get information first hand from the physicians so the marketing message can be adjusted. This will help to improve sales and reach a wider audience more efficiently.

Internal Delays in NPL

The estimated costs of having in the BCC a person from US depends on the length of his/her stay. Usually the NPL takes at least nine months. Taking travelling costs, wage, expatriate bonus and accommodation, etc. into account, the estimated costs for nine months (one launch) are sixty-five thousand dollars.

The projected gains can be achieved by saving on cancellation fees thanks to avoiding the delays and by saving on one fulltime equivalent and US will be more aware of BCC's issues during the NPL in the EU. Moreover, the key person from US can be assigned to other improvement projects described further in this chapter and that is why the costs of the key person are divided according to the participation on the different projects.

Marketing Collaterals

Based on the estimation of working hours spent on the creating of the list of the most effective marketing materials divided by the type of launched product, which is 40 hours, and on the average wage mentioned already at the beginning of this chapter, the forecasted costs are two thousand four hundred dollars.

The forecasted gains can be achieved by saving time on deciding which marketing materials to use and by avoiding the use of the marketing materials that are not effective. Better choice of collaterals also reduces their storing and transportation costs.

IFU

In the previous proposition on how to avoid internal delays, the costs involved in having a key person from US enrolled in the product launch were are already described. The projected costs of creating stricter contracts for translators in each country of EU are limited because the contracts already exist and only need certain corrections, which could higher the costs slightly. However, this would be countered by having higher quality translations, which would reduce the costs of potential lawsuits and reduce the risk of delay due to poor quality of the translations. The costs of creating a smaller document with the essential information would be covered by US, who creates all marketing materials in English. The BCC covers costs for translations and printing the materials. The storing and the transportation costs will hire the cost of the smaller IFU as well.

The gains are achieved by higher sales through better customer satisfaction and general improvement of St. Jude Medical's image.

Operations

The involvement of the key person from US that would be involved in the NPL process, its costs and gains were already described in this chapter at two different improvements projects. Furthermore, the US will be able to create more realistic image of the EMEAC market needs and priorities and this will enable SJM to achieve a more rational division of the new products over the different market.

The gains will arise from reducing the risk of strategic back orders in EMEAC and consequently raising customer satisfaction and sales.

Service

The SPOC will be rationalized per regions or countries within EU. In total, there can be approximately seventeen SPOCs. The costs comprise of the costs of their identification and also of part of the wage equal to the time of the employee(s) spent on managing the communication flows. Hiring more field technical engineers would be very expensive and that is why SJM should better rationalize the location of current FTEs.

The gains are achieved by an increase in service level towards the customer. Consequently, the more satisfied customer will be willing to pay a higher price for the products within the SJM portfolio.

The forecasted costs and gains of all proposed improvements are displayed in the chart on the next page. If SJM would implement all the alternatives, the total savings in one year and a half would be hundred twenty-eight thousands five hundred dollars. If not all alternatives would be implemented, then the two best options would be creating the awareness campaign and US key person participation on projects and launches.

Table 13: Forecasted Costs and Gains (Q3 2011 – Q4 2012)

COSTS

FORECAST ($)		Managing employees SPOC	Managing employees WIKIPEDIA	Awareness Campaign	Internal Delays US key person	Marketing Collaterals	IFU US key person	IFU Better contract	IFU Smaller IFU	Operations US key person	Service SPOC	TOTAL
2011	Q3	3 000	3 000	7 500	11 000	1 200	3 600	5 000	0	7 000	0	41 300
	Q4	1 000	3 000	7 500	10 000	1 200	4 000	5 000	5 000	7 600	5 000	49 300
2012	Q1	1 000	0	10 000	8 400	0	5 000	3 000	2 000	8 200	7 000	44 600
	Q2	1 000	0	10 000	7 300	0	5 300	0	3 000	9 000	7 000	42 600
	Q3	1 000	0	12 000	11 000	0	3 600	3 000	3 500	7 000	7 000	48 100
	Q4	1 000	0	12 000	10 000	0	4 000	3 000	3 500	7 600	7 000	48 100
TOTAL COSTS		8 000	6 000	59 000	57 700	2 400	25 500	19 000	17 000	46 400	33 000	274 000

GAINS

FORECAST ($)		Managing employees SPOC	Managing employees WIKIPEDIA	Awareness Campaign	Internal Delays US key person	Marketing Collaterals	IFU US key person	IFU Better contract	IFU Smaller IFU	Operations US key person	Service SPOC	TOTAL
2011	Q3	0	0	0	11 000	0	1 000	0	0	1 000	0	13 000
	Q4	1 300	0	0	11 000	0	1 000	3 000	0	1 000	0	17 300
2012	Q1	1 500	1 000	20 000	11 000	1 500	2 000	4 500	3 000	18 000	9 000	71 500
	Q2	1 700	2 000	22 000	11 000	1 500	4 000	5 000	6 000	27 000	10 500	90 700
	Q3	1 800	2 500	28 000	11 000	1 500	6 000	6 600	7 000	25 000	11 000	100 400
	Q4	1 800	3 000	35 000	11 000	1 500	8 000	7 300	9 000	22 000	11 000	109 600
TOTAL GAINS		8 100	6 000	105 000	66 000	6 000	22 000	26 400	25 000	94 000	41 500	402 500

SAVINGS

FORECAST ($)		Managing employees SPOC	Managing employees WIKIPEDIA	Awareness Campaign	Internal Delays US key person	Marketing Collaterals	IFU US key person	IFU Better contract	IFU Smaller IFU	Operations US key person	Service SPOC	TOTAL
2011	Q3	-3 000	-3 000	-7 500	0	-1 200	-2 600	-5 000	0	-6 000	0	-28 300
	Q4	300	-3 000	-7 500	1 000	-1 200	-3 000	-2 000	-5 000	-6 600	-5 000	-32 000
2012	Q1	500	1 000	10 000	2 600	1 500	-3 000	1 500	1 000	9 800	2 000	26 900
	Q2	700	2 000	12 000	3 700	1 500	-1 300	5 000	3 000	18 000	3 500	48 100
	Q3	800	2 500	16 000	0	1 500	2 400	3 600	3 500	18 000	4 000	52 300
	Q4	800	3 000	23 000	1 000	1 500	4 000	4 300	5 500	14 400	4 000	61 500
TOTAL SAVINGS		100	2 500	46 000	8 300	3 600	-3 500	7 400	8 000	47 600	8 500	128 500

Table 13: The Forecasted Costs and Gains (Q3 2011 – Q4 2012)

CONCLUSION

The book, Marketing Strategy for Medical Devices Market, was based on the author's experience during her internship in the regional EMEAC headquarters of an American Fortune 500 company St. Jude Medical in Brussels, Belgium. SJM is a global medical company that develops medical technology with the focus on the treatment of cardiac, neurological and chronic pain diseases and thus the four major areas of activity are cardiac rhythm management, atrial fibrillation, cardiovascular and neuromodulation. The internship was done at the atrial fibrillation marketing department and therefore the book was focused on the marketing strategy for medical devices of the AF portfolio designed for treatment irregularities of the heart beat.

The aim of the book was to describe and optimize where possible a launch plan strategy on the European Union market for the ViewFlex™ PLUS ICE ablation catheter and the ViewMate™ Z Intracardiac Ultrasound Console (mapping system) of the Atrial Fibrillation portfolio belonging to the American company St. Jude Medical. The aim was reached in three steps. Firstly, after establishing a theoretical background, the analytical part of the book described the current launch strategy of SJM. Secondly, the critical points during the launch procedure were identified and described into detail. In the final part of the book, propositions for improvements for some of the critical points were made and described, including forecasted costs and gains.

Marketing strategies of medical devices for medical markets are very complex and specialized partially as the buyers are not the final users (patients) but the professionals (physicians and hospitals) and also due to the fact that the medical device market is a high competitive place with only few strong players. SJM as any other medical company has to make a lot of afford in order to draw the core buyers' attention and acknowledgement. The physicians acknowledgement is important especially during the new product launch when the physician becomes the "Key opinion leader" of the launched product. It is essential in the highly niche market of the Medical industry where the recommendations by peers plays a crucial role. This primary focus on the physician rather than on the patient is mirrored in the SJM's brand promise: "More control. Less risk.". SJM has a big network of physicians supporting their products, however this network needs to be maintained and broadened whenever possible. This is primarily done through participation on congresses and trade shows, providing education for physicians in the SJM Advanced Learning Centers, ensuring excellent service and the personal relationship of the sales representatives with the physicians. Equally, as described in the propositions, a greater problem awareness can be created and thus leading to more efficient marketing and reaching a wider audience. All these factors have a direct impact on the market share and revenues of SJM and can change them significantly.

Besides the above mentioned strategy, the launch process itself can be made more cost-effective. Gains can be made by exploiting possible synergies with the US both on the operational as on the strategic level. This will help limiting the risk of delays and managing competing interest between the two sales regions, US and ID. Furthermore, the communication flows, both internally (between the employees) and externally (with the customers), can be managed improved by a small number of improvements. These changes would lead to the more clear communication channels, reducing the internal costs and improving the service and image towards the customer. Lastly a rationalizing of the marketing materials will save costs internally (transportation and storage) and will enable SJM to reach the healthcare professionals more efficiently.

Thus, the contribution of the book for SJM lies firstly in the provision with the clear overview of the critical activities during the new product launch and secondly in the proposition for improvement. The propositions can make the marketing strategy more efficient, improve the weak points that are currently causing problems and delays and this way avoid going up in price during the next launches.

REFERENCES

[1]   *A3cc.com* [online]. 2010 [accessed 2011-02-20]. Do You Know Your ROAI?. Available on: <http://www.a3cc.com/roai.aspx>.

[2]   BEHE, Bridget; DUDEK, Tom. *Harrells.com* [online]. 2010-06-03 [accessed 2011-03-01]. For Some, The Price Is Right. Available on: <http://harrells.com/blog/for-some-the-price-is-right/>.

[3]   BERKOWITZ, Eric N., et al. *Marketing*. 6th ed. US: Irwin/McGraw-Hill, c2000. 736 p. ISBN 0-07-116830-3.

[4]   *Businessplans.org* [online]. c1994-2011 [accessed 2011-02-13]. Strategic Marketing Plan. Available on: <http://www.businessplans.org/market.html>.

[5]   *Cardioassoc.com* [online]. 2011 [accessed 2011-03-19]. Catheter Ablation. Available on: <http://www.cardioassoc.com/patient_pgs/procedures/catheterabl.asp>.

[6]   *Cardiotek.com* [online]. Sep 29, 2010 [accessed 2011-02-05]. CardioTek - The Maastricht EP system. Available on: <http://www.cardiotek.com/>.

[7]   *Ce-mark.com* [online]. 2009 [accessed 2011-04-03]. CE Marking Medical Devices. Available on: <http://www.ce-mark.com/cemd.html>.

[8]   CHURCHILL, Gilbert A., et al. *Sales Force Management*. 6th ed. US: Mc Graw-Hill Higher Education, c2000. 727 p. ISBN 0-07-027555-6.

[9]   *Crbard.com* [online]. 2011 [accessed 2011-04-25]. BARD Advancing the Delivery of Healthcare[®]. Available on: <http://www.crbard.com/>.

[10] *Eur-lex.europa.eu* [online]. 1993 [accessed 2011-03-05]. Council Directive 93/42/EEC. Available on: <http://eur-lex.europa.eu/LexUriServ/LexUriServ.do?uri=CELEX:31993L00 42:EN:HTML>.

[11] FREISNER, Tim. *Marketingteacher.com* [online]. c2000-2011 [accessed 2011-02-19]. Marketing Budget. Available on: <http://marketingteacher.com/lesson-store/lesson-marketing-budget.html>.

[12] *Ge.com* [online]. 2011 [accessed 2011-03-05]. GE Healthcare Overview: Women's Healthcare, Surgery, Healthcare Financing: Available on: <http://www.ge.com/products_services/healthcare.html>.

[13] GOLIA, Nathan. Marketing medical devices. *Dmnews.com* [online]. 2008-11-24, [accessed 2011-03-26]. Available on: <http://www.dmnews.com/marketing-medical-devices/article/121283/>.

[14] HORÁKOVÁ, Helena. *Strategický Marketing*. Praha: Grada Publishing, c2000. 152 p. ISBN 80-7169-996-9.

[15] *Internal materials.*

[16] KOTLER, Philip. *A Framework for Marketing Management*. 2nd ed. Upper Saddle River, New Jersey, US: Pearson Education, Inc., c2003, 2001. 363 p. ISBN 0-13-100117-5.

[17] KOTLER, Philip. *Kotler on Marketing: How to Create, Win, and Dominate Markets*. New York, US: The Free Press, c1999. 257 p. ISBN 0-684-85033-8.

[18] KOTLER, Philip. *Marketing Insights from A to Z: 80 Concepts Every Manager Needs to Know*. Hoboken, New Jersey, US: John Wiley & Sons, Inc., c2003. 206 p. ISBN 0-471-26867-4.

[19] KOUYOUMDJIAN-GURUNLIAN, Sarin. Hitting the Bull's Eye in Medical Device Marketing. *Prurgent.com* [online]. 2010-06-11, [accessed 2011-03-21]. Available on: <http://www.prurgent.com/2010-06-11/pressrelease100559.htm>.

[20] MACHKOVÁ, Hana, et al. *International Marketing*: Theory, Practices and New Trends. 1st ed. Praha: Oeconomica, c2010. 192 p. ISBN 978-80-245-1643-1.

[21] *Nhlbi.gov* [online]. 2009 [accessed 2011-03-12]. Cardiac Heart Arrhythmias. Available on: <http://www.nhlbi.nih.gov/health/dci/Diseases/arr/arr_whatis.html>.

[22] RACKHAM, Neil. *SPIN®-Selling*. New ed. Farnham, Surrey, UK: Gower Publishing Limited, 2009. 233 p. ISBN 978-0-566-07689-3.

[23] *Siemens.com* [online]. 2011 [accessed 2011-03-04]. Siemens Global Website. Available on: <http://www.siemens.com/entry/cc/en/#188200>.

[24] *Sjm.com* [online]. c2011 [accessed 2011-03-08]. St. Jude Medical, Inc. Available on: <http://www.sjm.com/>.

[25] WALKER, Jr., Orville C.; BOYD, Jr., Harper W.; LARRÉCHÉ, Jean-Claude. *Marketing Strategy: Planning and Implementation*. 2nd ed. US: Irwin/McGraw-Hill, c1996. 392 p. ISBN 0-256-13692-0.

[26] *Who.int* [online]. 2003 [accessed 2011-04-05]. Medical Device Regulations. Available on: <http://www.who.int/medical_devices/publications/en/MD_Regulations.pdf>.

LIST OF USED ABBREVIATIONS

AF	Atrial Fibrillation
BCC	Brussels Coordination Centre
CRM	Cardiac Rhythm Management
CRT	Cardiac Resynchronization Therapy (Device)
DBS	Deep Brain Stimulation
EMEAC	Europe, Middle East, Africa, Canada
EP	Electrophysiology
FLM	Field Leadership Meeting
FMR	Full Market Release.
FTE	Field Technical Engineer
ICD	Implantable Cardioverter Defibrillator
ICE	Intracardiac Echocardiography
ID	International Division
IFU	Instruction for Use
LMR	Limited Market Release.
Marcom	Marketing communication
MRI	Magnetic Resonance Imaging.
MS	Market share
NMD	Neuromodulation
NPL	New product launch
RF	Radio-frequency
SJM	St. Jude Medical
SPOC	Single Point of Contact
ST segments	Electrical changes between hearbeats
US	United States of America

LIST OF APPENDIXES

Appendix nb. 1:   AF Product Portfolio (15)

Appendix nb. 2:   Global Presence of St. Jude Medical (15)

Appendix nb. 3:   Organization Structure (From Sales Division to the Physician)

Appendix nb. 4:   Brochure (15)

Appendix nb. 5:   Sell Sheet (15)

Appendix nb. 6:   Advertising (15)

Appendix nb. 7:   Spec Sheet (15)

Appendix nb. 8:   Evaluation Form (Catheter Performance) (15)

APPENDIXES

Appendix nb.1: AF Product Portfolio

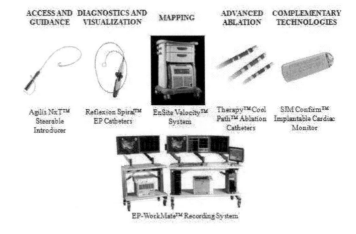

ACCESS AND GUIDANCE	DIAGNOSTICS AND VISUALIZATION	MAPPING	ADVANCED ABLATION	COMPLEMENTARY TECHNOLOGIES
Agilis NxT™ Steerable Introducer	Reflexion Spiral™ EP Catheters	EnSite Velocity™ System	Therapy™ Cool Path™ Ablation Catheters	SJM Confirm™ Implantable Cardiac Monitor

EP-WorkMate™ Recording System

Appendix nb.2: Global Presence of St. Jude Medical

CORPORATE HEADQUARTERS	☆ TECHNOLOGY PLATFORMS	● MANUFACTURING US	International	◆ REGIONAL HEADQUARTERS (Geographic Divisions)
St. Paul, Minnesota, US	St. Paul, MN (Cardiovascular, AF)	Arizona	Brazil	Hong Kong (Asia Pacific)
	Sylmar, California (CRM)	California	Israel	Brussels, Belgium (EMEAC)
	Plano, Texas (Neuromodulation)	Minnesota	Malaysia	Tokyo, Japan (Japan)
		New Jersey	Sweden	Sao Paolo, Brazil (Latin America)
		Oregon	Thailand	Austin, Texas (US)
		Puerto Rico	Costa Rica	
		South Carolina		
		Texas		

Appendix nb.3: Organization Structure (From Sales Division to the Physician)

Appendix nb.4: Brochure

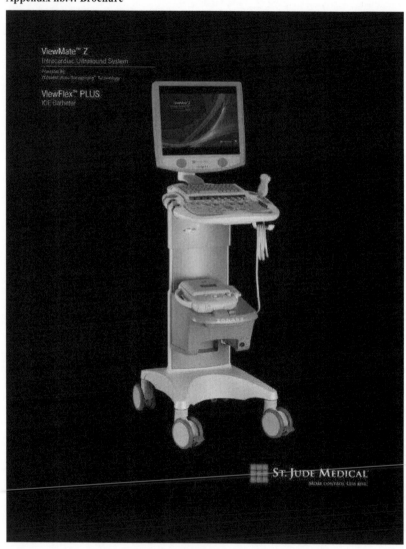

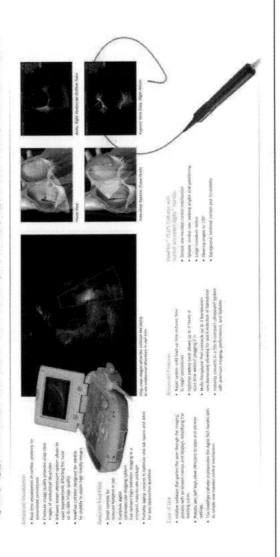

System Safety

- Catheter interface module designed to isolate the patient from the system to enhance patient safety
- Automatic system shut down when catheter temperature threshold is reached
- Fully featured system allows flexibility in imaging across a wide range of modalities (TEE, Transthoracic, Color Doppler, etc)

ViewFlex PLUS ICE Catheter Specifications

Feature	Specification
Catheter size	9 F
Introducer size	10 F
Insertable length	90 cm
Steering	Anterior/Posterior ≤ 120 degree flexion
Transducer type	64 element phased array
Viewing sector	90 degrees

ViewMate Z System Specifications

Feature	Specification
Dimensions	
System Cart	69H x 20.1W x 28.2D (in) 157H x 51W x 72D (cm)
Ultrasound Engine	2.9H x 9.8W x 9.9D (in) 7.3H x 25W x 25D (cm)
Weight	
System Cart	144 lb (65 kg)
Ultrasound Engine	5.5 lb (2.49 kg)
Display – System Cart	
Monitor	19 in (48 cm) High resolution color LCD mounted on articulating arm
Pixel Resolution	1280 x 1024
Display – Ultrasound Engine	
Monitor	5.8 in (15 cm) High resolution color LCD
Pixel Resolution	800 x 480

ATRIAL FIBRILLATION   CARDIAC RHYTHM MANAGEMENT   CARDIOVASCULAR   NEUROMODULATION

Global Headquarters
One St. Jude Medical Drive
St. Paul, Minnesota 55117
USA
+1 651 756 2000
+1 651 756 3301 Fax

Atrial Fibrillation Division
One St. Jude Medical Drive
St. Paul, Minnesota 55117
USA
+1 651 756 2000
+1 651 756 3301 Fax

St. Jude Medical Coordination Center BVBA
The Corporate Village
Da Vincilaan 11 Box F1
1935 Zaventem
Belgium
+32 2 774 68 11
+32 2 772 83 84 Fax

St. Jude Medical Brazil, Ltda.
Rua Itapeva, 538
7º ao 9º andares
01332-000 - São Paulo (SP)
Brasil
+55 11 5080 5400
+55 11 5080 5429 Fax

St. Jude Medical (Hong Kong) Limited
Suite 1608, 16/F Exchange Tower
33 Wang Chiu Road
Kowloon Bay, Kowloon
Hong Kong SAR
+852 2996 7688
+852 2956 0622 Fax

SJMprofessional.com

ST. JUDE MEDICAL
MORE CONTROL. LESS RISK.

Appendix nb. 5: Sell Sheet

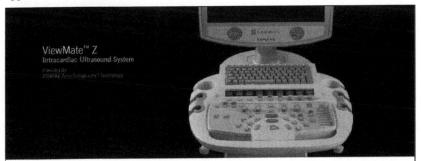

ViewMate™ Z
Intracardiac Ultrasound System

Powered By
ZONARE Zone Sonography Technology

EXCEPTIONAL, REAL-TIME VISUALIZATION
FOR PRECISE INTERVENTIONAL AND EP PROCEDURES

The ViewMate Z System is a fully contained ICE system designed for exceptional, real-time image guidance and visualization of anatomical structures. The system delivers fast, high fidelity imaging performance to help clinicians increase confidence when performing complex electrophysiology procedures while providing a reduced footprint in the EP lab.

Exceptional Visualization

- Real-time imaging streamlines electrophysiology procedures
- Premium image quality provides crisp clear images of anatomical structures
- Software based ultrasound system allows for rapid upgrades providing the most up-to-date image quality

Simplified Operation

- On-screen menus and displays help guide clinicians through the imaging process
- Presets and soft keys allow clinicians to save and retrieve settings effortlessly
- System recognition of transducer parameters optimize menu displays simplifying the learning curve
- Rapid boot-up time reduces time to begin procedures

Zone Sonography™ Technology

Conventional

Zone Imaging

Line-by-line data acquisition limits image processing and formation. Zone

Zone Technology decreases image acquisition time while improving image quality

Converts from a fully-featured cart based system into a 5 ½ lb hand-held system without sacrificing performance.

ST. JUDE MEDICAL
MORE CONTROL. LESS RISK.

Small footprint and light weight system designed for effortless maneuverability and maximum versatility in tight or crowded spaces

- 5 inch (13 cm) diameter full swivel wheels with dual shock resistant front and back wheels.
- Front wheels with switchable brake and direction lock
- Multi-Transducer Port (MTP) – up to three transducers connected simultaneously
- One handed release of Scan Engine from cart
- Monitor mounted high-fidelity stereo speakers

- Integrated front handle for transport and position
- Saddle bag storage bins
- 5 ½ lb Ultrasound Engine
- ViewFlex Catheter Interface module
- Transthoracic transducer
- Optional 3 hour battery pack

Ordering Information

Reorder Number	Product Description
100044000	ViewMate Z System
100044271	ViewMate Z System with battery pack
100042294	Transesophageal Transducer
100042298	Continuous Wave Transducer
100042741	Linear Transducer
100043997	ViewMate Cart Battery Pack
100043998	Audio Video Extension Device
100043999	ECG Accessory Cable

ATRIAL FIBRILLATION   CARDIAC RHYTHM MANAGEMENT   CARDIOVASCULAR   NEUROMODULATION

Global Headquarters
One St. Jude Medical Drive
St. Paul, Minnesota 55117
USA
+1 651 756 2000
+1 651 756 3301 Fax

Atrial Fibrillation Division
One St. Jude Medical Drive
St. Paul, Minnesota 55117
USA
+1 651 756 3000
+1 651 756 3301 Fax

St. Jude Medical Coordination Center BVBA
The Corporate Village
Da Vincilaan 11 Box F1
1935 Zaventem
Belgium
+32 2 774 68 11
+32 2 772 83 84 Fax

St. Jude Medical Brazil, Ltda.
Rua Frei Caneca, 1380
7° ao 9° andares
01307-002 - São Paulo (SP)
Brazil
+55 11 5080 5400
+55 11 5080 5423 Fax

St. Jude Medical (Hong Kong) Limited
Suite 1608, 16/F Exchange Tower
33 Wang Chiu Road
Kowloon Bay, Kowloon
Hong Kong SAR
+852 2996 7486
+852 2956 0622 Fax

SJMprofessional.com

ST. JUDE MEDICAL
MORE CONTROL. LESS RISK.

Appendix nb. 6: Advertising

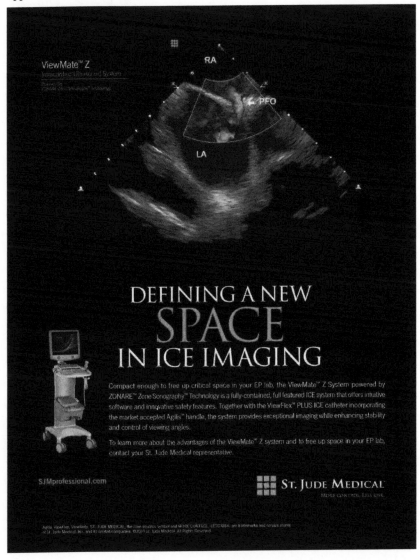

Appendix nb. 7: Spec Sheet

ViewMate™ Z
Intracardiac Ultrasound System
Powered By
ZONARE Zone Sonography™ Technology

ViewFlex™ PLUS
ICE Catheter

The ViewMate™ Z System is a fully contained ICE system designed for exceptional, real-time image guidance and visualization of anatomical structures. The system delivers fast, high fidelity imaging performance to help clinicians increase confidence when performing complex electrophysiology procedures while providing a reduced footprint in the EP lab.

SYSTEM FEATURES

- Multi-Transducer Port (MTP) - up to three transducers connected simultaneously
- One-handed release of Engine from Cart for portable scanning
- Integrated front handle for transport and position
- Saddle bag storage bins
- Monitor mounted hi-fidelity stereo speakers
- 5 in (13 cm) diameter, full swivel wheels with dual shock resistant front and back wheels
- Front wheels are switchable brake and direction lock
- Power cord wrap features

CART DIMENSIONS

Height
- Maximum operational: 62 in (157 cm)
- Minimum operational: 50.5 in (128 cm)
- Display lowered for transport: 41 in (104 cm)

Width
- 20.1 in (51 cm)

Depth
- 28.2 in (72 cm)

Weight
- 144 lb (65kg)

9" Display Monitor
- Pixel resolution: 1280 x 1024
- High resolution LCD screen mounted on articulating arm
- 0.294 mm pixel pitch
- Viewing angle (H/V): 178 degrees typical
- Minimum 400:1 contrast
- +/- 120° horizontal rotation
- 30° backward tilt
- Full 90° forward tilt into secure transport position

SCAN ENGINE DIMENSIONS

Height
- 2.9 in (7.3 cm)

Width
- 9.8 in (25 cm) - including handle

Depth
- 9.8 in (25 cm)

Weight
- 5.5 lb (2.49 kg) - with battery

5.8" Display Monitor
- Pixel resolution: 800 x 480
- High resolution LCD screen
- 0.16 mm pixel pitch

ST. JUDE MEDICAL
MORE CONTROL LESS RISK

Site Requirements

- 100 - 130 VAC, 50 - 60 Hz or 200 - 260 VAC, 50 - 60 Hz
- 442W (1512 BTU/hr)
- Ambient air temperature of 0° - 35° Celsius
- Ambient relative humidity of up to 80% non-condensing

Media (Removable)

- Configurable formats: DICOM uncompressed, DICOM RLE
- Removable USB memory stick media for transfer to a PC
- Support for ShowCase Viewer burning to export media
- Ability to export images in non-DICOM format

Imaging Modes

- 2-Dimensional
- M-Mode
- Pulsed wave
- Tissue doppler imaging
- Continuous wave
- Color doppler

Storage Capacity

Cart: 250 GB

- DICOM uncompressed: ~300,000 images
- DICOM RLE: ~1,000,000 images

Scan Engine: 2 GB

- DICOM uncompressed: 1,280 images
- DICOM RLE: 4,060 images

Connections

- HDMI Connector
- (4) USB Ports
- Ethernet (10/100 Base T)
- Wireless capable via bridge
- Optional audio video extension device AVED
    - DVI input
    - DVI to external display
- VGA out, S-Video Out, Composite Video Out
- Analog Audio Out
- TOSLINK (digital audio) Out

ATRIAL FIBRILLATION   CARDIAC RHYTHM MANAGEMENT   CARDIOVASCULAR   NEUROMODULATION

Global Headquarters
One St. Jude Medical Drive
St. Paul, Minnesota 55117
USA
+1 651 756 2000
+1 651 756 3301 Fax

Atrial Fibrillation Division
One St. Jude Medical Drive
St. Paul, Minnesota 55117
USA
+1 651 756 2000
+1 651 756 3301 Fax

St. Jude Medical Coordination Center BVBA
The Corporate Village
Da Vincilaan 11 Box F1
1935 Zaventem
Belgium
+32 2 774 68 11
+32 2 772 83 94 Fax

St. Jude Medical Brazil, Ltda.
Rua Frei Caneca, 1380
7° ou 8° andares
01307-002 - São Paulo (SP)
Brazil
+55 11 5080 5400
+55 11 5080 5401 Fax

St. Jude Medical (Hong Kong) Limited
Suite 1608, 16/F Exchange Tower
33 Wang Chiu Road
Kowloon Bay, Kowloon
Hong Kong SAR
+852 2996 7688
+852 2956 0622 Fax

SJMprofessional.com

ST. JUDE MEDICAL
MORE CONTROL. LESS RISK.

Appendix nb. 8: Evaluation Form (Catheter Performance)

ST. JUDE MEDICAL
MORE CONTROL LESS RISK

Evaluation Form

Evaluation number: _____

Procedure Information

Please print clearly

Physician: _____ Date: _____

Hospital: _____ Location (City/Country): _____

SJM Rep/FCE: _____ Catheter reorder #: _____

Type of procedure: A Flutter ☐   AF ☐   VT ☐   Other: _____

Irrigated Ablation Catheter Most Commonly Used

Cool Path Duo ☐   Cool Path ☐   Celsius ThermoCool ☐   Navistar ThermoCool ☐   EZSteer ThermoCool ☐

Other: _____

Product Performance (check one rating for each characteristic)

Characteristic	Excellent	Above Average	Average	Below Average	Poor
Visibility of tip on fluoroscopy					
Stability of catheter tip when in contact with cardiac tissue					
Tactile feedback of tip to tissue contact					
Tip conformance to tissue					
Signal quality					
Far field rejection					
Efficacy of therapy delivery					
Speed of ECG signal reduction during ablation					
Overall catheter performance					

Procedural Settings

Generator used: SJM T series ☐   Stockert ☐   EPT ☐   Other: _____

Highest power used: 25W ☐   30W ☐   35W ☐   40W ☐   45W ☐   50W ☐

Average power used: 25W ☐   30W ☐   35W ☐   40W ☐   45W ☐   50W ☐

Irrigation pump used: SJM Cool Point ☐   Cool Flow ☐   Other: _____

Flow setting used during ablation: _____ ml/min

Evaluation

What do you think is the biggest benefit of this product? _____

_____

_____

Please return completed form to +32 2 774 6939

104